LET'S
MAKE
PRESENTS

100 Gifts for Less than $1.00

LET'S MAKE PRESENTS

100 Gifts for Less Than $1.00

by ESTHER HAUTZIG

ILLUSTRATED BY AVA MORGAN

Thomas Y. Crowell Company: NEW YORK

With love and gratitude to my parents

A Word to Boys and Girls

It is great fun to give, and to receive, presents. And the pleasure is greatest of all if the presents are things you have made yourself.

In this book I have tried to describe to you presents that you can make inexpensively and easily, presents that are useful, pretty and appropriate for the different members of your family and for some of your friends. Before you proceed with the actual making of any of the gifts described in this book, read the pages entitled "Before You Begin."

GOOD LUCK AND GOOD GIVING:

A Word to the Parent

This book is intended for children, but perhaps a word or two with you will help boys and girls to make the gifts suggested here.

This word to the parent is a plea! If you can possibly stand more clutter, try to save for, and with, the children boxes of all shapes, sizes, and descriptions. As you will see, a shoe box can be transformed into a pretty sewing kit, and an empty soup or vegetable can may be reincarnated, we hope, as an elegant pencil holder. Scraps of fabric, felt, ribbon, wool, pretty paper, and magazine pictures are used in many of the gifts, so do bear with the children when they save these bits and pieces. Old magazines are a menace in any room where order and lack of dust are desired, to be sure; but you might suggest on a rainy day that the youngsters clip those pictures that they can use and make them throw out the rest of the magazines.

I have earnestly tried to make the directions for constructing all the gifts as explicit and detailed as possible. However, there may be times when your child will need a word of advice, or just a pat on the back and a bit of encouragement.

All the presents were tested with and without children and they all proved to be fun to make and pretty to look at. Let us hope that you, your family, and your friends will be the lucky recipients of many handsome and useful gifts in the months and years to come.

Contents

GIFTS FOR CHILDREN AND TEEN-AGERS

GIFTS FOR THE WHOLE FAMILY

GOOD THINGS TO EAT

Before You Begin

Before you start to make a present, think carefully about the person for whom you want to make it. Try to remember what his favorite colors are, what his interests are, what he does in his work. By forming a clear picture of each person for whom you are making a present, you will make it easier to decide on what to make for him or for her.

Collect odds and ends of fabrics, ribbon, decorative paper, boxes, beads, sequins, pretty magazine pictures, cardboard, and so on. Put them neatly in boxes in the corner of your closet, in the family room, in the basement, or anywhere else in the house where they won't create a mess and annoy, your mother.

When you want to make a gift for someone, look at the table of contents of this book and also look in your odds-and-ends boxes to see what you have there. Often you will find that you will not need to go out and buy anything at all to make a gift. Your odds-and-ends collection is likely to turn out to be a gold mine of useful items.

Some of the gifts in this book call for initials to be painted or embroidered. You will find a complete alphabet that you can trace on page 182.

Before you start making any of the gifts described in this book read through all the directions given for making it, from beginning to end. Get together all the materials and tools you are going to need before you start making it. It is a nuisance to have to stop in the middle of making something and go looking for a scrap of wool or a bottle of glue. Have everything ready and in front of you before you begin.

It is advisable to follow all the directions given for making the various gifts very carefully and precisely. However, there are some gifts in this book which can be made an inch bigger or an inch smaller than indicated, such as the pajama case, the throw pillow, the place mats, and a few others. Some of the suggestions for color combinations may not be your favorite colors or the favorite colors of the person to whom you will give the present. Don't let that stop you. Use the color combinations you prefer, or the yarns and fabric you have in your collection. The whole idea of *making* a gift is that it represents not only your thoughtfulness and affection for the person you are giving it to, but also your taste, workmanship, and ingenuity. For instance, if you do not have red felt for the Apple Pajama Case, but do have purple felt on hand, call it a Plum Pajama Case.

You can also adapt the illustrations suggested for decorating many of the gifts. You need not copy the illustrations *exactly* as they appear in the book. The illustrations will guide you, but use your own ingenuity or imagination when you put the designs into the gifts you will be making. Perhaps you will come up with variations of the gifts suggested here and they may be even nicer and easier to make than the ones in the book. If you care to let me know about them, I should be happy to hear from you.

When you use glue, don't slop it on in great quantities. Dip the brush into the glue until all the bristles are well covered. Remove excess glue by moving the brush bristles back and forth against the edge of your glue container. Put the glue on the wrong side of the paper or fabric with short, even strokes. Be sure that the glue reaches to all the edges of the paper or fabric. It isn't enough to have glue in the middle only, because glue doesn't spread by itself. When you are finished using the glue, cover the glue jar tightly, for it dries out quickly.

If you are going to use any paints, be sure that you spread plenty of old newspapers over your working surface. This is easier to do than to have to clean up paint spots with soap and water, or even turpentine. Make sure that your brush has been properly dipped in the paint and all excess paint removed; then paint with short, even strokes. Immediately after you finish the painting, wash your brush. Use a little turpentine or benzine poured into an ashtray or any small glass container. Or use plain hot water and lots of soap. Dry the brush and put it away, wrapped in a piece of newspaper.

Be careful when you use scissors, knives, or razor blades. When you cut a large piece of paper or fabric with scissors, put the material down on the table, or other working surface, and hold one hand over it, not under it, to keep it in place. When using a razor blade or knife, always cut away from yourself so an unexpected jerk of your hand will not result in your cutting yourself.

Clean up all the scraps of fabric, paper, or other material immediately after finishing your work. Save those odds and ends that you can use again, and throw out the completely unusable bits right away.

Wrapping your gift may be as important a part of presenting it as the making of it was. Wrappings need not be costly productions. Fold plain white tissue paper neatly over your object or box, hold it in place with small pieces of gummed tape, not yards of it, and paste a pretty picture on it or tie it with a ribbon or cord. If the object you have to wrap is unwieldy, such as the Magazine Holder, or the Mobile, use crepe paper, which is very flexible and comes in large sheets. You can always put the unwieldy object in the middle of a large piece of crepe paper and gather the ends with a rubber band or pretty ribbon. Use gummed tape or gummed stickers for sealing, and tie the ribbon in as neat a bow as you can.

LET'S
MAKE
PRESENTS

100 Gifts for Less than $1.00

Sewing Hints and Stitches

1. NEEDLES. For sewing fabrics like cotton, rayon, linen, terry cloth, you should use a number 7 milliner's needle. For sewing felt, denim, or canvas, use a number 3 or 4 needle, with a large eye, because you will use a heavier thread or wool yarn.

2. THREAD. For felt fabrics use wool yarn of any weight except the very heavy worsted wool used for making bulky sweaters. For other fabrics use a number 50 cotton or mercerized thread. When you use embroidery yarn, 3-ply is the average thickness required, but you can use 4- or even 6-ply if you want your embroidery pattern to stand up higher. Always use a piece of thread that is about 18 to 20 inches long. Cut it off with scissors from the spool or ball. *Don't bite it off*. To thread a needle, hold the eye of the needle against a light and push one end of the thread through it.

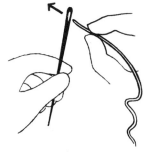

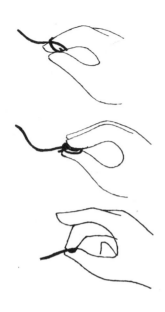

3. TO MAKE A KNOT. Take the end of a piece of thread between the forefinger and thumb of your left hand, then wind the thread once around the end of your forefinger and roll the forefinger and right thumb together. Slip the thread off the finger and pull it with the left hand. A small knot will form. You may need to repeat this for a larger knot. You can also start your sewing with a few backstitches sewn one over the other instead of a knot, just as you do when you are finished with a seam.

4. THIMBLE, SCISSORS, AND TAPE MEASURE. Buy a metal or plastic thimble that fits the middle finger of the hand you sew with. Scissors should be sharp. Pinking shears cut fabric with a sort of zigzag edge which does not unravel. This is very convenient if you have to hem the fabric or make a seam, but pinking shears are not essential. Whenever you are about to cut anything for sewing or gluing, have your tape measure right near you. "Measure twice, cut once" is an old, old proverb, and a good proverb it is.

5. IRONING. If the gift that you have sewed needs ironing, use a medium hot iron and do the ironing on the wrong side of the fabric, if you can, or put a piece of cloth over it first. Don't let the iron stand on the fabric for more than a second. Move the iron back and forth, with firm, even movements.

6. RUNNING STITCH. Begin sewing this stitch with three or four little stitches sewn one over the other, instead of making a knot in the thread. The running stitch itself is a small, even stitch, running on a straight line. Try to make each stitch about $\frac{1}{8}$ inch long, though if it is closer to $\frac{1}{4}$ of an inch no thunder or lightning are going to strike you. You can run up to six of these little stitches on the needle and then pull the needle through the fabric. Finish your seam with three or four little stitches sewn one on top of the other.

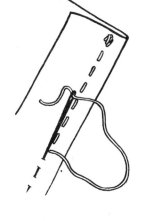

7. BACKSTITCH. Begin sewing this stitch with three or four little stitches sewn one on top of the other. Make a little stitch backwards on the upper part of the two pieces of fabric you are sewing together, and then make a longer stitch forwards on the under part of the two pieces of fabric you are sewing together. Bring the needle back on the upper part of the two pieces of fabric where the last stitch ended and then push it forward again on the under part of the two pieces of fabric you are sewing. Do this until the seam is completely done and finish it with three or four small backstitches one on top of the other.

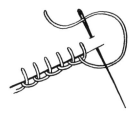

8. BLANKET STITCH. Make a knot at the end of your piece of thread. Put your needle in ¼ inch from the edge of the fabric, put the thread under the point of the needle and then pull the needle with the rest of the thread through. Repeat until finished.

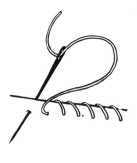

9. OVERCASTING STITCH. Make a knot at the end of your piece of thread. Point the needle away from the hand with which you are working and toward the shoulder of the other hand. The stitches should be about ¼ inch apart. End a row of overcasting stitches with a few little backstitches one over the other.

10. LONG AND SHORT BLANKET STITCHES. Make a knot at the end of your piece of thread. Put the needle in ¼ inch away from the edge of the fabric for the long stitch and ⅛ inch away from the short stitch. The stitches should be about ⅛ inch apart. End with a few little backstitches one over the other.

11. CHAIN STITCH. Make a knot at the end of your thread. Put the needle in the fabric as for a running stitch. When the point is through and the eye is still out, bring the thread under the point of the needle. Then draw the needle all the way through to form a loop. For the next chain stitch, and those after that, put the needle in right next to the place where the thread came out, bring the thread under it again to form a loop, and continue doing so until the chain stitch is done.

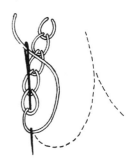

12. OUTLINE STITCH. Make a knot at the end of your thread. The outline stitch is done a little bit like a backstitch, but it is slanted. Make one slanted backstitch in front of another, letting each one overlap the one before it just a little bit, until the design is filled.

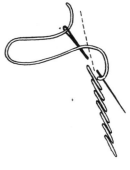
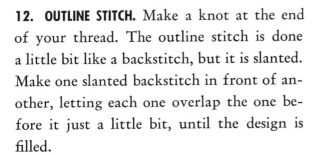

13. BASTING STITCH. This is not a permanent stitch. It holds two pieces of material. together while another, stronger, stitch is being sewn. Make a knot at the end of your thread. Make large running stitches, about ½ inch apart, on a straight line. End with a few backstitches, sewn one on top of the other. When your permanent stitches have been made, cut the basting stitches every few inches and pull out all the threads.

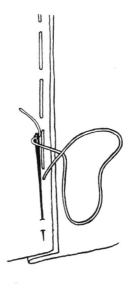

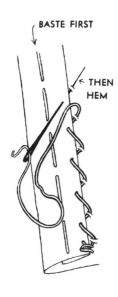

THEN
HEM

14. HEMMING. Hemming is done so that the rough edges of the fabric do not show. First fold under ½ inch of the fabric and press down the crease with your hand or press it against the edge of a table or working counter. Then fold the fabric again, ½ inch for a regular hem, 1 inch for a wide hem. Press down the second crease with your hand. Baste the fold about ¼ inch from the first fold. To sew the hem permanently make small, slanting stitches right near the first fold. Push your needle all the way through the folded fabric and just enough farther to get hold of a tiny piece of the right side of the fabric—the side that will show—and then push the needle back through the folded edge. Begin and end your hemming stitch with two or three little backstitches, one on top of the other.

FOLD
TWILL

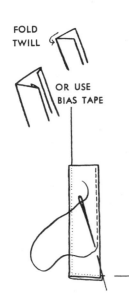

OR USE
BIAS TAPE

15. BINDING. Use either bias tape or regular twill or rayon tape. Bias tape is good for round, or rounded, pieces of fabric. Twill or rayon tape is good for binding straight pieces of fabric. Crease the piece of tape in the middle and put the edge of the piece of fabric that is to be bound between the folds of the tape. Sew on the tape, being sure to catch both sides of it, with a running stitch or backstitch. Begin and end with three or four little backstitches, sewn one on top of the other.

16. SHIRRING. Make a double or triple knot in your thread. If the thread is not too heavy, double it and then make a knot. Be sure the thread is long enough for the whole piece of fabric you are about to gather. About ¼ inch from the edge of the fabric, sew a fairly large running stitch, on a straight line. Leave at least 4 inches of thread free at the end of the row of sewing. About ¼ inch below this row make another row of running stitches and again leave 4 inches of thread free. Take the loose pieces of thread at the ends of the two rows of sewing in one hand and pull them very carefully and slowly, holding the fabric with the other hand so the threads can slide through. When you have gathered the fabric to the desired width, tie the loose threads several times and cut off the extra thread. Even out the folds neatly.

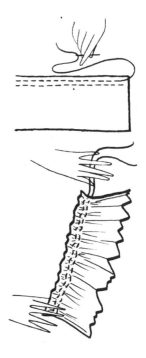

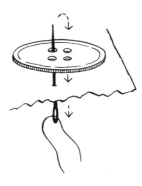

17. SEWING ON BUTTONS. First mark with chalk or pencil exactly where the buttons are to be sewed on. Thread your needle, double the thread, and make a double knot at the end. Put your needle through the fabric so that the knot is on the wrong side of it. Put the needle in one of the holes in the button and pull the thread through. Then put the needle in the opposite hole in the button. Repeat this process, sewing through the holes at least six times, and then fasten the thread on the wrong side of the fabric with a few little backstitches, one on top of the other.

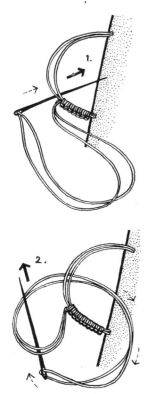

18. MAKING A BUTTON LOOP. Take a double piece of cotton thread, or a single piece of wool yarn, and make a double knot. Mark two places in the fabric—one where the loop will begin, the other where it will end. Put the needle through the fabric so that the knot is on the wrong side. Then put the needle through the other place, where the loop is to end, but do not pull the thread all the way through the fabric. Leave a loose piece of thread between these two places and fasten the loop on the wrong side with a few backstitches. Then with the thread and needle make little loop knots very close together over the loose piece of thread until it has been completely covered with loop knots and is nice and sturdy.

GIFTS FOR MOTHER, GRANDMOTHER, AUNT, AND OTHER LADIES

PRETTY HANDKERCHIEFS

3 white ladies' hankies from the 5-and-10-cent store
green and red embroidery thread
needle; pencil; tracing paper; scissors
four pins; tape measure

MAKE IT LIKE THIS:

• 1. Trace the illustration onto your tracing paper three times. You will need one traced illustration for each handkerchief. Draw the initial of the person who will receive this gift in the middle of the design (see alphabets in back of book).

• 2. Pin the traced design in the corner of each handkerchief, about one inch away from the hems.

• 3. Embroider the circle or flowers with an outline stitch (see instruction No. 12, in the front) and the leaves with a chain stitch (see instruction No. 11). Use an outline stitch to embroider the initial.

• 4. When the design is all embroidered, take out the pins and tear the paper off gently.

• 5. Repeat this on the other two hankies and you have a really nice gift with little effort and little cost.

INITIAL HERE

INITIAL HERE

COSMETICS CASE FOR POCKETBOOK

YOU WILL NEED:

8-by-13 inch piece of medium-weight fabric such as
   butcher linen, denim, or flannel
thread to match the fabric; one button
embroidery yarn to contrast with the fabric; needle;
   scissors; tape measure

MAKE IT LIKE THIS:

• 1. Hem the piece of fabric on all sides (see hemming instructions, No. 14, in the front of the book).

• 2. Fold the fabric in three parts, so that two parts measure 4 inches each and the third part measures 3 inches.

• 3. Sew the folded fabric with a blanket stitch (see instruction No. 8, in the front) as indicated in the illustration. Make a loop for the button, as shown in the illustration, in the center of the overlapping piece of fabric (see instruction No. 18). Sew on the button at the center of the bottom part of the folded fabric.

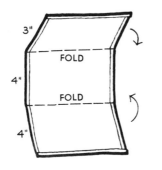

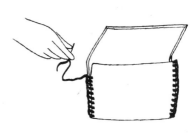

FLOWER HAT PIN

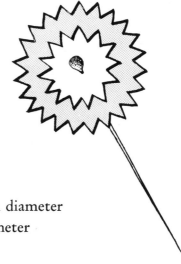

YOU WILL NEED:

    hatpin with pearl head
    1 circle of felt 1½ inches in diameter
    1 circle of felt 1 inch in diameter
    scissors

MAKE IT LIKE THIS:

• 1. Fold the first circle in half and then cut out petals so the felt looks like a flower. When both circles have been thus cut, put the smaller circle on top of the larger circle.

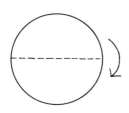 

• 2. Push the hatpin through the center of the circles of felt and push the circles all the way, close to the pearl head of the pin, so the hatpin head looks like the center of the flower. This will look nice on your mother's hat.

POT
HOLDER

YOU WILL NEED:

> 2 round scraps of decorative flannel, denim, or other
>   heavy cotton fabric about 8 inches in diameter
> 2 old wash cloths or good pieces of old toweling
> piece of ribbon, 5 inches long
> embroidery yarn; thread; bias tape
> scissors; tape measure; needle
> kitchen bowl, 8 inches in diameter
> chalk; tracing paper; pencil; pins

MAKE IT LIKE THIS:

• 1. Put the kitchen bowl on top of the decorative fabric and draw around it with chalk. Do the same with a double piece of old towel or two wash cloths. Then cut the material where it is marked with chalk.

• 2. Put one circle of decorative fabric on the table, then the two circles of toweling, and last the other circle of decorative fabric. Baste them all together (see instruction No. 13, in the front of the book).

• 3. Sew the bias tape around the basted circles with a back-

stitch (see instruction No. 7). Be sure the needle catches both sides of the tape.

• 4. Transfer with pencil the illustration of a cooking pot to your tracing paper. Pin the tracing paper in the center of the circle and embroider the outline of the pot with a running stitch (see instruction No. 6). Be sure the needle and thread go through all the layers of fabric, because then the embroidering will also quilt the material. When the embroidery is done, take out the pins and gently tear off the tracing paper.

• 5. Fold the 5-inch length of ribbon in half and sew it on the edge of the pot holder so it can be hung on a kitchen hook.

SMALL SHOULDER SHRUG

YOU WILL NEED:

old shirt, man's or lady's, sports or white
2 yards of colored fringe from 5-and-10
thread; scissors; needle; tape measure

MAKE IT LIKE THIS:

• 1. From the back of the shirt, cut out a triangle of fabric that measures about 30 inches on the side marked A in the illustration and 19 inches on the sides marked B and C.

• 2. Hem the triangle of fabric (see instruction No. 14, in the front of the book).

• 3. Sew on the fringe all around the triangle of fabric, using a backstitch (see instruction No. 7). Then the shrug is done.

If you use a white shirt, sew on a colored fringe. This will look very pretty worn over a pastel, or print, summer dress. If you use a sports shirt made of patterned fabric, use a fringe of a solid color, matching one of the colors in the shirt.

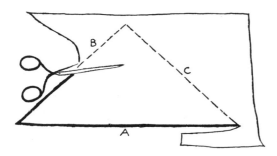

FRAGRANT PINCUSHION

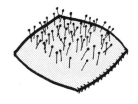

YOU WILL NEED:

    a 6-by-3-inch piece of cotton or flannel fabric
    2 or 3 fragrant closet sachets
    thread to match fabric
    box of pins with multicolored heads
    scissors; needle; tape measure

MAKE IT LIKE THIS:

• 1. Fold the piece of fabric in half, so it measures 3 by 3 inches. Sew sides A and B together on the wrong side with a backstitch (see instruction No. 7, in the front). Leave side C unsewn.

• 2. Slip the fragrant sachets in through side C. Sew up side C with a small, neat, running stitch (see instruction No. 6). Put in pins, with multicolored heads, all over the pincushion, and wrap it. Your favorite lady's sewing basket is going to be sweet smelling indeed!

BATH MITTEN

YOU WILL NEED:

    a piece of terry cloth, or an old terry towel
    thread to match; piece of ribbon
    pencil; paper; scissors; needle; pins

MAKE IT LIKE THIS:

• 1. Put your hand down flat on a piece of paper, keeping your thumb separate from the other fingers. Trace around your hand with pencil, but make your tracing much bigger than your hand since the bath mitt will be used by people with large, and small, hands. Cut out the pattern and pin it to the terry cloth.

• 2. Cut the fabric around the paper. Take out the pins and pin the pattern on another piece of terry cloth. Cut that out, too. Now you have two pieces.

• 3. Sew the two pieces together with a backstitch (see instruction No. 7, in the front of the book). Turn it inside out.

• 4. Fold the piece of ribbon in half and sew it on in the place marked A. The bath mitten, when hung in the bathroom, can be used to save little pieces of soap.

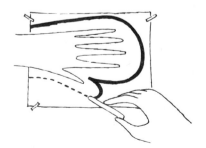

DECORATIVE HANGERS

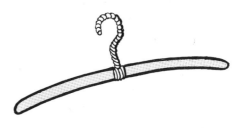

YOU WILL NEED:

    4 wooden hangers

    felt fabric; gummed tape

    tape measure; pencil; scissors; needle; thread

MAKE IT LIKE THIS:

• 1. Cut the felt into eight pieces, each of which should be 8 by 3 inches, and fold each piece in half lengthwise.

• 2. Sew together two of the open sides of each piece with a backstitch (see instruction No. 7, in the front). Repeat this until you have all eight pieces of felt sewn into felt tubes. To turn the tubes inside out so that the seams don't show, hold a tube in your left hand and with your right hand push the eraser end of the pencil against the end seam until it is on the inside.

• 3. Slip two tubes on each hanger. The tubes will meet at the middle. Cover the wire part of the hanger with gummed tape by winding it round and round so that the wire doesn't show. Then wind the tape around the hanger where the two pieces of felt met so that you don't see the ends of the felt. When you have done this on all four hangers, your gift is all finished.

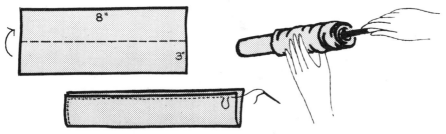

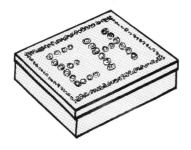

JEWELRY
BOX

empty box made of wood, metal, or sturdy paper (such
as candy and cookies come in)

scraps of felt fabric

enamel paint in your favorite color

glue; scissors; tape measure

MAKE IT LIKE THIS:

• 1. Glue the felt that you have cut to the right sizes to the
inside of the box. The felt will protect jewelry from being
scratched.

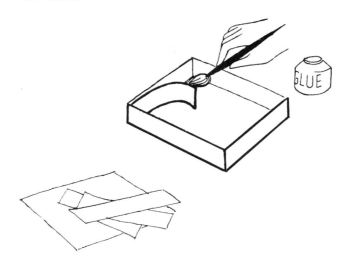

• 2. Paint the outside of the box and the cover, inside and out-side, with enamel paint in your favorite color.

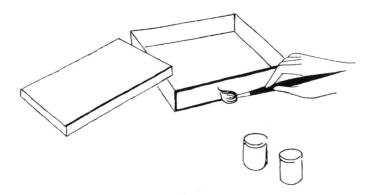

• 3. To decorate the box, glue on top of it sea shells, buttons, or beads in the shape of the initials of the person to whom you will give the box.

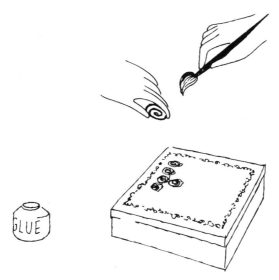

TERRY-CLOTH COBBLER'S APRON

YOU WILL NEED:

one terry bath towel, old or new
20½ inches of bias tape to match towel
2 buttons
thread to match towel
scissors; tape measure; needle; thimble

MAKE IT LIKE THIS:

• 1. Fold the towel across the width, 16 inches from one end.

• 2. Cut a 10-inch slit along the folded line of the towel. Bind it with the bias tape, using an overcasting stitch (see instruction No. 9, in the front of the book).

• 3. Sew the two buttons at A and B and make loops for the buttons at C and D (see instruction No. 18).

• 4. Make a pocket for holding soap, wash cloth, and so on, by folding over a 4-inch piece of towel at the bottom and sewing it with a running stitch (see instruction No. 6) at the sides of the towel and in the middle. This is a perfect apron for bathing a baby, doing laundry at the sink, or washing dishes.

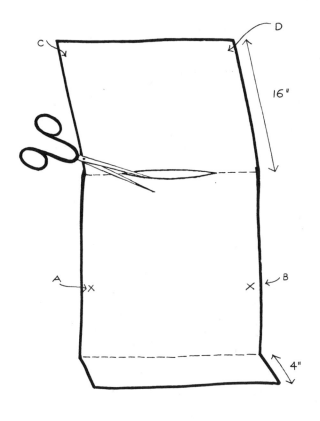

C

D

16"

A →X

X ← B

4"

BIAS TAPE

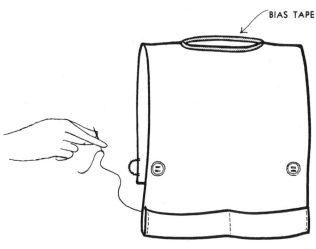

25

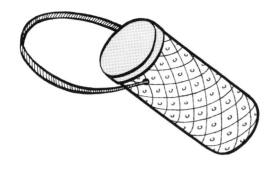

KNITTING
BOX

YOU WILL NEED:

> round cereal box (the 18-ounce Quaker Oats box is
>   perfect)
> decorative paper
> rayon or cotton cord
> show-card paint; glue
> tape measure; brush; paper punch

MAKE IT LIKE THIS:

• 1. Shake the cereal box clean of all cereal.

• 2. Cut the piece of decorative paper to cover the outside of
the box (7 by 14 inches is just right for the Quaker Oats box).
Put glue on the wrong side. Put the container in the center of
the paper and glue the paper on.

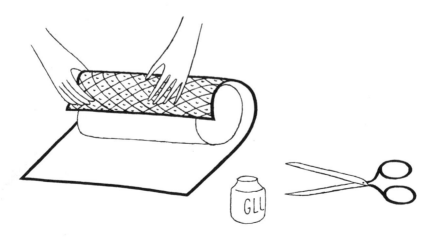

• 3. Paint the lid of the box with paint that either matches or contrasts with the colors in the decorative paper.

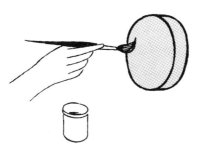

• 4. About two inches from the top of the box, punch one hole on one side of the box and another just opposite the first hole. Make a big knot at one end of the rayon or cotton cord, and pull the other end through one hole, from the inside. Pull this end through the other hole, from the outside, and make another big knot. Then the knitting box is finished.

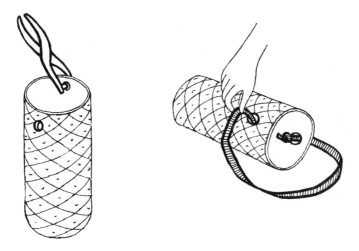

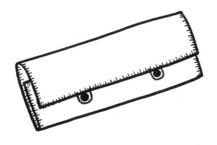

GLOVE
CASE

YOU WILL NEED:

> 1 man's handkerchief
> 2 decorative buttons
> colored embroidery thread
> needle; scissors; tape measure

MAKE IT LIKE THIS:

• 1. Make a border with a long and short blanket stitch (see instruction No. 10, in the front) around the whole handkerchief.

• 2. Sew buttons at A and B, 6 inches apart, and make two loops (see instruction No. 18) at C and D also 6 inches apart. Be sure the loops are large enough for the buttons.

• 3. Fold the handkerchief in three parts and close it by putting the buttons through the loops. Press the two folds with the palm of your hand (see that it's clean) so the glove case lies flat. You can also take it in both hands and press the folds along the edge of a table.

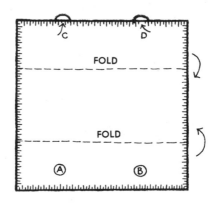

SWEATER
GUARD

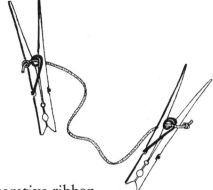

YOU WILL NEED:

    2 toy plastic clothespins
    15 inches of very narrow decorative ribbon
    thread to match
    needle; scissors

MAKE IT LIKE THIS:

• 1. Pull the ribbon through the holes formed by the wire in the centers of the clothespins. Make knots at each end of the ribbon so it won't pull out. You may need to roll the ends of the ribbon a bit, to make them thinner, in order to get them through the holes. That's all there is to this one, and it will keep the sweater from sliding if it is worn over the shoulders.

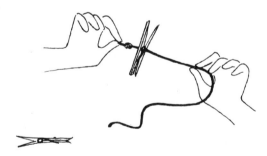

RECIPE
FILE

YOU WILL NEED:

> notebook, 8½ by 11 inches
> decorative paper
> 2 pieces of ribbon, each 8 inches long
> glue; colored pencil
> scissors; tape measure

MAKE IT LIKE THIS:

• 1. Paste two pages together on two sides (marked A and B in drawing) and leave side C open. Repeat this until you have 24 "envelopes" in the notebook. Mark each envelope with the kind

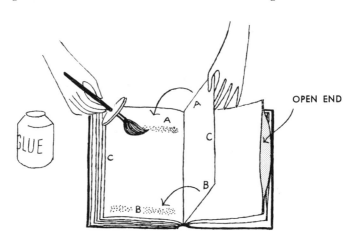

of recipes to be kept there—Appetizers, Soups, Meats, Fish, Vegetables, Desserts, Drinks, Sandwiches, etc.

• 2. Glue the pieces of ribbon onto the center of the back and

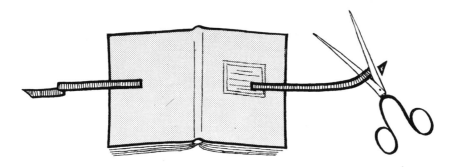

front covers of the notebook and glue decorative paper onto the covers. Cut the ends of the ribbon on the bias, to prevent fraying. You can make the same file for patterns, bills, or personal letters.

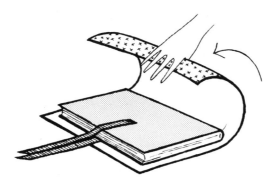

VEIL HAT

⅞ yard of veiling

1¼ yards of very narrow velvet ribbon of approximately the same shade as the veiling

thread to match the ribbon and veiling

scissors; needle

MAKE IT LIKE THIS:

• 1. If the lady to whom you will give this elegant head covering has dark hair, choose a light veiling such as beige, blue, or red. If she has light hair, a black, dark brown, or navy-blue veil hat should become her. Be gentle with the veiling when you sew it. Veiling is not sturdy and requires care in handling. Your patience will be amply rewarded when the veil hat is finished.

• 2. Fold the veiling in half and sew the ends together. It will

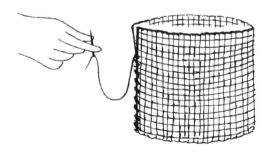

look like a cylindrical spider web. Shirr it at the top with a running stitch (see instruction No. 6, in the front) and pull threads at A and B so that the top is closed.

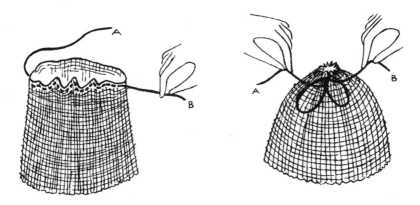

• 3. Cut the velvet ribbon into six 7-inch pieces and make little bows.

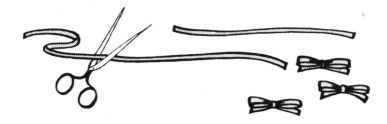

• 4. Sew on the bows every 1½ or 2 inches on the seam of the veil, which will be in the back. Then it's ready and you'll be ever so glad! So will the recipient of your gift.

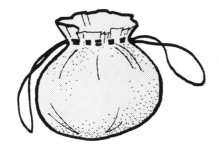

POCKETBOOK

YOU WILL NEED:

a circular piece of felt fabric, about 25 inches in diameter

a circular piece of cardboard, about 6 inches in diameter

30 inches of grosgrain ribbon, either matching or in contrast to the color of the felt

scissors; tape measure; razor blade in holder

chalk; safety pin; glue

MAKE IT LIKE THIS:

• 1. Glue the piece of cardboard to the center of the piece of felt.

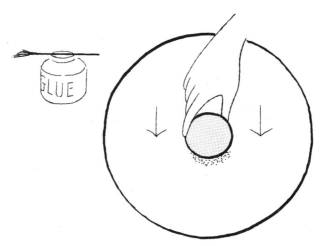

• 2. Cut little slits 1½ inches from the edge of the felt for pulling through the ribbon which will be used to close the bag. To do this, chalk-mark a ½-inch slit about every 2 inches until you have 26 marks. Cut through the marks with the razor blade. Be sure that you have a pile of old newspapers or magazines about 2 inches high under the felt so you don't cut the surface of the area on which you are working.

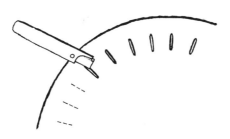

• 3. Attach the safety pin to one end of the ribbon and pull it through the slits. Sew the ends of the ribbon together, fill the bag with crushed tissue paper so it looks nice and full, and your gift is ready.

POMANDER
BALLS

YOU WILL NEED:

> 2 oranges
> whole cloves (can be bought in boxes in grocery stores or supermarkets)

MAKE IT LIKE THIS:

• 1. Stick the cloves very closely one next to another into each of the oranges. The cloves will protect the oranges from spoiling and make them look ever so different. It takes a while to get the oranges all covered with the cloves, so be patient. The pomander balls, when done, last for many years, and are worth all the effort you've put in to get them done.

• 2. The oranges with the cloves will give a lovely aroma to any closet or drawer where they are put and they will be a most unusual and different gift. They keep away moths and are therefore perfect for putting in a drawer with woolen garments.

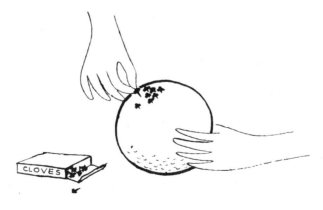

HANDKERCHIEF CASE

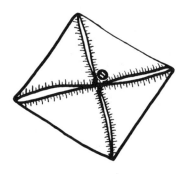

YOU WILL NEED:

> one large man's handkerchief
> colored thread
> decorative button
> needle; scissors

MAKE IT LIKE THIS:

• 1. Make a border with a long and short stitch (see instruction No. 10, in the front) around the whole handkerchief.

• 2. In corner A sew on your decorative button.

• 3. In corners B, C, and D sew a loop (see instruction No. 18) large enough for the button to go through easily.

• 4. Fold the handkerchief so that all the corners meet in the middle. Your ladies' handkerchief case is all finished and ready to be given to the lucky lady.

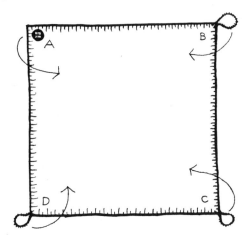

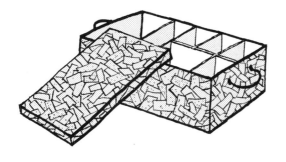

SEWING BOX

empty shoe box; heavy yarn or cord
scraps of gift wrapping paper
small boxes, of any size
rubber cement, or other glue
nail and hammer, or paper punch
scissors; tape measure; shellac; brush

MAKE IT LIKE THIS:

• 1. Glue decorative paper all over the shoe box and the cover in patchwork-quilt fashion. The scraps of paper can overlap one another, be upside down or right side up. Put a coat of shellac all over the box.

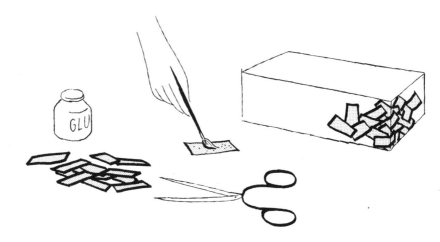

• 2. Cover the insides and outsides of the bottoms of smaller boxes (a cheese box, kitchen match box, for instance) with scraps of gift wrapping paper also in patchwork-quilt fashion and see where they fit into the shoe box. Glue them into the box. They will hold yarn spools, small scissors, thimble, and other sewing tools.

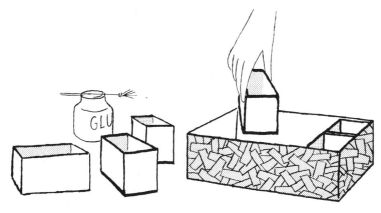

• 3. About 2 inches from the top of the box, in the middle of each side, punch out two holes about 3 inches apart, for the handles of the box. Pull through two lengths of heavy yarn or cord and on the inside make triple or quadruple knots.

The box is then finished. If you have money to spare, buy some yarn spools, a thimble, a package of needles, and two or three skeins of embroidery yarn.

SHOPPING
BAG

YOU WILL NEED:

> ½ yard of denim
> 1 ⅓ yards of grosgrain ribbon
> 8 buttons
> thread; tape measure; scissors; needle

MAKE IT LIKE THIS:

• 1. Cut the denim 18 by 36 inches. Hem one of the 36-inch edges (see instruction No. 14, in the front). Fold it in half and, on the wrong side, sew together the A and B sides with a back-stitch (see instruction No. 7).

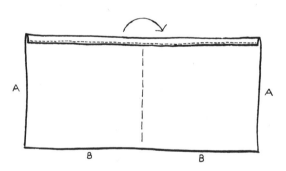

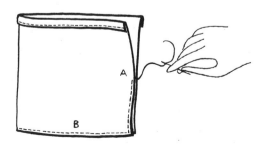

• 2. Cut the grosgrain ribbon into four 12-inch pieces. Hem both ends of each piece.

• 3. For the shopping bag handles, sew two pieces of the ribbon together, using a backstitch (see instruction No. 7) leaving 1½ inches on each side unsewn. Do the same with the other two pieces of ribbon.

• 4. Sew the handles with a backstitch (see instruction No. 7) very securely on each side of the bag.

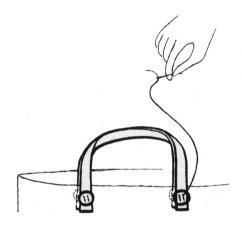

• 5. To make handles stay firmly attached to the bag, sew a button on each end of the handle, on the inside and outside of bag. Be sure you repeat the stitches in sewing on the buttons at least twelve times for each two holes. The bag is going to hold, sometimes, heavy things and you will want to make sure that the handles are firmly sewn to the bag.

CASE
FOR
GLASSES

YOU WILL NEED:

> piece of felt, about 6 by 7 inches
> package of paper for cleaning glasses
> gold, silver, or colored thread
> scissors; tape measure; needle; chalk

MAKE IT LIKE THIS:

• 1. Cut the felt into two pieces, 3 by 7 inches each.

• 2. In the center of one of the pieces of felt, sketch with chalk, but very lightly, the initials of the person to whom you will give this gift. Embroider the initials with a chain stitch (see instruction No. 11, in the front).

• 3. Sew the pieces of felt together on three sides with a blanket stitch (see instruction No. 8). One side will remain unsewn, for the glasses to be put in.

• 4. When you are finished, put in the case a package of Sight-Saver papers, sold in all drugstores and dime stores, so that the recipient of the gift can clean the glasses.

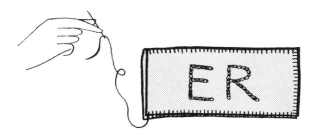

SEA-SHELL
EARRINGS

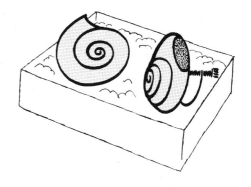

YOU WILL NEED:

> 2 sea shells, not larger than ¾ inch in diameter
> 2 earring clips or screws, from 5-and-10
> tweezers; Duco cement

MAKE IT LIKE THIS:

• 1. Put the two sea shells on the table, with their backs facing you. Squeeze out a few drops of Duco cement onto the shells.

• 2. Using the tweezers, pick up the sea shells and put them very gently on top of the earring clips or screws, right in the center. Let the cement dry. Pack the earrings in a small box. It would be nice if you put some fresh white cotton in the bottom of the box, to highlight the earrings.

KITCHEN APRON

YOU WILL NEED:

> 1 dish towel (16 by 31 inches) and 1 wash cloth
> 2 yards of 2-inch ribbon
> thread to match the towel
> scissors; tape measure; needle; pins

MAKE IT LIKE THIS:

• 1. Shirr one 31-inch side of the dish towel so that it is only 16 inches wide. (See instruction No. 16, in the front, and pull the thread a little after each 10 stitches.) You can adjust the width when you have sewn the whole side. Be sure your thread is about 30 inches long.

• 2. Find the middle of the side of the dish towel which has been shirred. Use your tape measure. Fold your ribbon in half and, with a pin, fasten the middle to the middle of the dish towel.

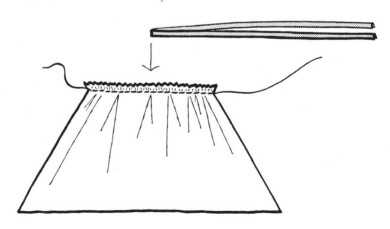

• 3. With your hand, press a crease lengthwise down the middle of the ribbon. Pin the ribbon to the dish towel until you reach the edges of the dish towel on both sides of the center. Sew it with a backstitch (see instruction No. 7), making sure that the ribbon is sewn on both sides of the dish towel. The ends will be used for tying the apron.

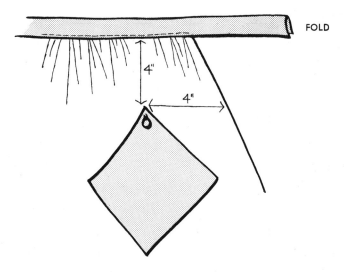

• 4. Using the tape measure, find a spot that is 4 inches from the top and 4 inches from the side of the apron.
• 5. On this spot sew one corner of the wash cloth with chain stitches (see instruction No. 11) repeated one on top of the other at least six times. Now you have an apron, with a built-in hand-wiper.

CORSAGE
OF
FLOWERS

YOU WILL NEED:

scraps of wool yarn of various colors
pencil with rubber eraser tip
scissors

MAKE IT LIKE THIS:

• 1. Put a piece of green wool along the length of a pencil, holding it firmly with thumb and forefinger. This will make the stem of the flower.

• 2. For the flower petals, wind a piece of red, yellow, purple, blue, or any color wool yarn about twenty times around the width of the pencil. Hold one end of the yarn with the thumb which is holding onto the green piece of wool for the stem.

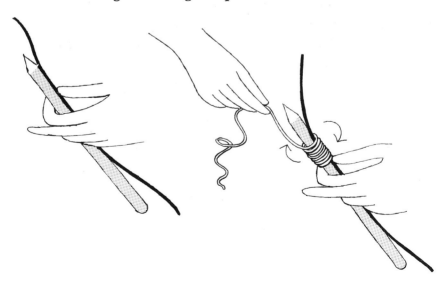

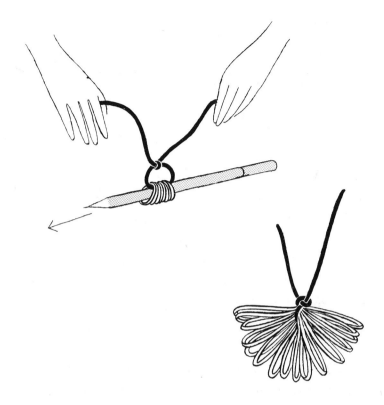

• 3. When you have made twenty turns around the pencil, hold the other end of the wool which is used for the flower petals with your forefinger.

• 4. Gently release the piece of green wool held by the thumb and forefinger and tie the ends together. Slip the pencil out from the petal loops and tighten the knot of the stem. Repeat this procedure until you have about ten flowers. Make the stems for the flowers of slightly varying lengths, so that the corsage will not be all stems and a bunch of flowers hanging limply at the end.

COMB CASE

YOU WILL NEED:

> scraps of felt
> contrasting or matching wool yarn and thread
> sequins or beads
> needles: 1 regular No. 7 needle and 1 needle with a large eye; pins
> scissors; tape measure; white chalk

MAKE IT LIKE THIS:

• 1. Cut the felt into two 5-by-2-inch pieces. On one piece, draw with chalk the initials of the person to whom you will give this. Sew the sequins or beads on top of the chalk marking.

• 2. Sew both pieces together on three sides with an overcasting stitch (see instruction No. 9, in the front) and leave one end open for slipping the comb in and out.

GIFTS FOR FATHER, GRANDFATHER, UNCLE, AND OTHER GENTLEMEN

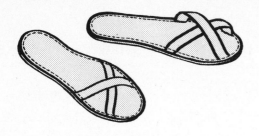

FELT
SCUFFS

YOU WILL NEED:

> cardboard (size depends on the size of slippers)
> felt (size also depends on the size of slippers)
> thread to match the felt
> scissors; needle; tape measure; pencil; chalk

MAKE IT LIKE THIS:

• 1. Put a pair of shoes of the person for whom you are making the scuffs on the cardboard. Trace around them with a pencil. Cut out the cardboard, which will make the soles.

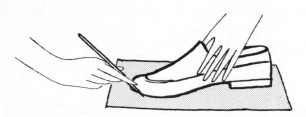

• 2. Put the cardboard on the felt and trace around it with chalk. Cut the felt ½ inch larger all around than the cardboard.

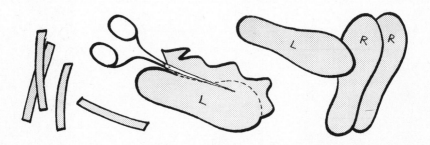

Mark two pieces of felt for the left foot and two pieces of felt for the right foot.

• 3. Cut four strips of felt 1 inch by 8 inches. Sew two of the strips, crisscross fashion, to one of the pieces of felt for the right foot, and two strips to one of the pieces of felt for the left foot. One end of each strip should be sewn about 2 inches from the toe of the felt sole. The other end of each strip should be sewn about 6 inches from the toe, using a backstitch (see instruction No. 7, in the front).

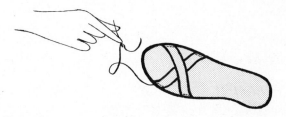

• 4. Place the cardboard sole on top of the piece of felt without the crisscross strips first, then place the piece of felt with the crisscross strips on top of the cardboard, for both the left and right foot. Sew around the felt with a blanket stitch (see instruction No. 8). Your gift is ready.

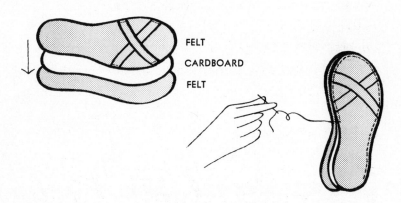

FELT

CARDBOARD

FELT

RUBBER BAND HOLDER

YOU WILL NEED:

> one plastic basket (stores pack tomatoes, berries, etc. in them)
> piece of cardboard
> scraps of multicolored ribbon
> scissors; safety pin; tape measure

MAKE IT LIKE THIS:

• 1. To transform a plain little plastic basket into a good-looking desk accessory, you will have to weave multicolored ribbons in and out of the holes all around the basket. Measure the basket all around and cut the ribbons about 6 inches longer, so you can tie a bow.

• 2. Attach a safety pin to one end of a piece of ribbon and weave it in and out of the holes all around the basket. Tie the ends into a bow. Repeat this until all the rows of holes have been covered with ribbon.

• 3. Cut a piece of cardboard to fit the bottom of the basket and put it in the basket. Fill the basket with colorful, or just plain, rubber bands and present it to someone who wants his desk to look handsome.

MAGAZINE HOLDER

YOU WILL NEED:

wire hanger; gummed tape; bottle cork, optional

MAKE IT LIKE THIS:

• 1. Bend the wire hanger as indicated on the illustration.
• 2. Cover the hanger entirely with gummed tape, and insert the end (C) into the center of the cork, if you have one. The cork will keep the holder from scratching table, desk, or floor when it stands with magazines held neatly in it. This holder is the perfect size for magazines the size of *Newsweek*, *Time*, and *Saturday Review*.

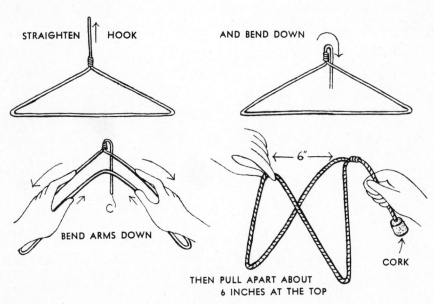

STRAIGHTEN HOOK AND BEND DOWN

BEND ARMS DOWN

THEN PULL APART ABOUT 6 INCHES AT THE TOP

6"

CORK

WORKSHOP ORGANIZER

YOU WILL NEED:

piece 16 by 27½ inches of very sturdy fabric: denim, canvas, sharkskin

thread to match the fabric

12 feet of ½-inch tape ribbon, matching or contrasting with the color of the fabric

16-inch stick, about ½ inch in diameter

strong needle; 2 thumbtacks

tape measure; scissors

MAKE IT LIKE THIS:

• 1. Hem the top and bottom of the fabric (see instruction No. 14, in the front). Make a 1-inch hem on top, so it will be roomy enough to push the stick through.

• 2. Fold the fabric so that you have a 10-inch-long double piece of fabric that looks like a pocket, with 5 inches of fabric on top. Sew the sides together with a backstitch (see instruction No. 7, in the front) and turn the fabric inside out.

• 3. Cut the ribbon into seven 15-inch pieces. (The remainder of the ribbon you will use for hanging the organizer.) Turn under ½ inch of each piece of ribbon at each end. Sew the ribbons onto the pocket 2 inches apart, thus dividing it into eight convenient compartments. Begin at the edge of the fabric and end also at the edge of the fabric. At the top the ribbon should be sewn on just under the 1-inch hem and it should end directly at the bottom of the fabric.

• 4. Push the stick through the 1-inch hem. With thumbtacks, attach the rest of the piece of ribbon to the ends of the stick. This organizer will be very useful for a workshop, to keep pliers, hammer, screwdriver, and other small tools always in place. This is also useful in the kitchen.

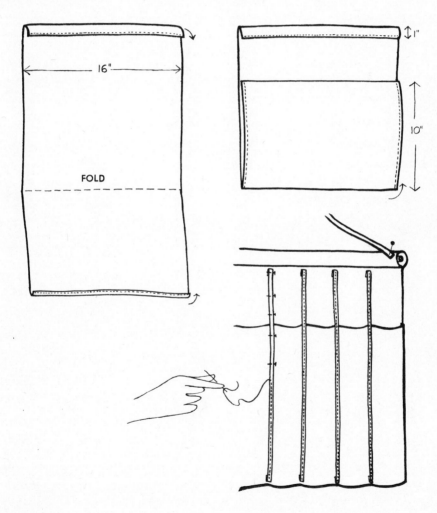

DIARY-APPOINTMENT BOOK

YOU WILL NEED:

> a 6-by-9-inch appointment book from a stationery store
>   or 5-and-10-cent store
> a piece of felt about 19 by 9 inches
> ready-made initials (available in notions stores and at
>   notions counters in department stores)
> thread to match the fabric
> rubber cement, or other glue
> scissors; tape measure; needle

MAKE IT LIKE THIS:

• 1. Cut the felt 19 by 9 inches. With long and short blanket stitches (see instruction No. 10, in the front) edge all four sides.

• 2. Spread glue evenly on the felt. Put the spine of the ap-

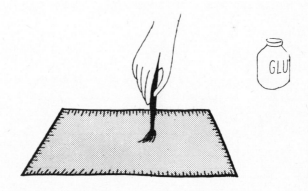

pointment book in the middle of the piece of felt and slowly raise the felt first on one side and then on the other for each cover of the appointment book. About 3 inches of felt should be glued onto the inside covers of the appointment book.

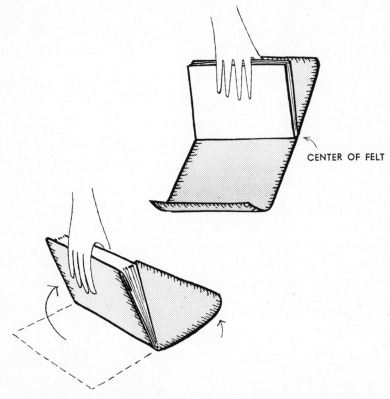

CENTER OF FELT

• 3. In the center of the cover, glue on the ready-made initials as a finishing touch for this useful gift for office or home.

SNAPSHOT
FRAME

YOU WILL NEED:

> cardboard, 15 by 5 inches
> 2 pieces of felt, each 16 by 5 inches
> 3 snapshots
> wool thread in contrasting color
> needle with large eye
> scissors; tape measure; mucilage or rubber cement; chalk

MAKE IT LIKE THIS:

• 1. Cut the cardboard into three pieces, each 5 by 5 inches. Paste one snapshot on each piece.

• 2. Arrange the three pieces side by side and lay one piece of felt over them. Leave ½ inch between the pieces of cardboard,

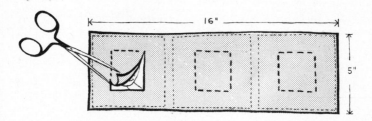

since the felt is 1 inch wider than the three pieces of cardboard. Mark with chalk either an oval or square shape where the felt is to be cut out to show the snapshots. Cut out these pieces of felt. Sew a long-and-short blanket-stitch border around each hole (see instruction No. 10, in the front) using the pretty wool thread.

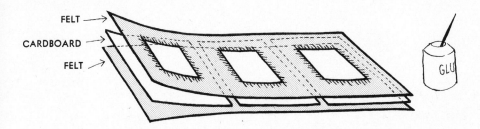

• 3. Glue the felt with the holes over the cardboard so the snapshots show through. Glue the other piece of felt to the back of the three pieces of cardboard. Sew a running stitch (see instruction No. 6) in places marked A and B in the illustration and then the frame is ready.

PHOTO ALBUM

YOU WILL NEED:

2 pieces of heavy cardboard, each 8½ by 11 inches

24 pieces of light cardboard, construction paper, or regular paper, each 8½ by 11 inches

2 loose-leaf rings

nail polish; blue show-card paint

old newspapers; paper punch; brush

MAKE IT LIKE THIS:

• 1. Put newspapers on the surface where you will be working. Paint the two loose-leaf rings with red nail polish. Let the polish dry and give the rings another coat of nail polish. Let that dry too.

• 2. Punch two holes in the 2 pieces of heavy cardboard and in the 24 pieces of lighter stock. The holes should be ½ inch from the edge of the paper and 2½ inches from the top and bottom of the page.

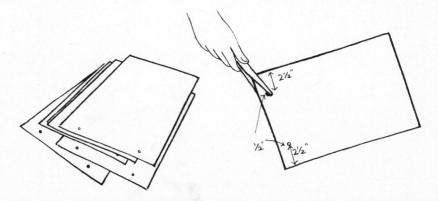

• 3. Paint the heavy cardboard with blue paint and let the paint dry. Using the nail polish, write OUR PHOTOGRAPHS in the center of one of the pieces of heavy cardboard.

• 4. Slip the rings through all the pieces of paper and the cardboard, making sure that the piece of cardboard without the writing is at the bottom and the piece with OUR PHOTO-GRAPHS written on it is on top. Get a package of photo corners, if you have the money, and you have a most useful and good-looking present.

BOOK HOLDER

YOU WILL NEED:

1 wire coat hanger; colorful gummed tape

MAKE IT LIKE THIS:

• 1. Bend the hanger as indicated on the illustration. Cover the wire with the gummed tape.

• 2. If you have a little money to spare, buy a paperback edition of a good novel or non-fiction work to give with this book holder. This is a good present for someone sick in bed; the patient will appreciate not only the book but also this prop to hold the book up. The book holder can also be used for propping up a book on the desk.

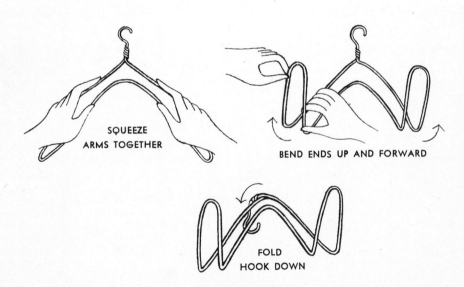

SQUEEZE ARMS TOGETHER

BEND ENDS UP AND FORWARD

FOLD HOOK DOWN

BOOKMARK

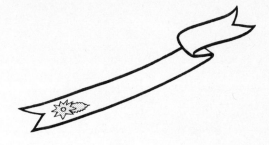

YOU WILL NEED:

>   10 inches of 1½ -inch grosgrain ribbon
>   picture of a flower
>   scissors; glue

MAKE IT LIKE THIS:

• 1. Cut out triangles from the ends of the grosgrain ribbon.

• 2. Find a small picture of a flower in a magazine, or in an old birthday or other greeting card. Cut it out and paste the picture at one end of the grosgrain ribbon. That's all there is to it and the result is very pretty.

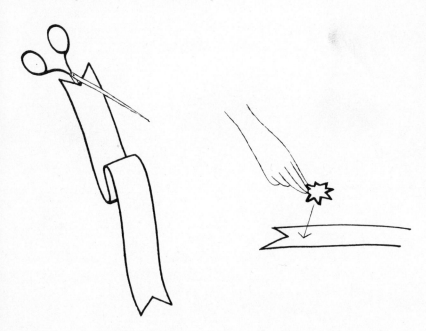

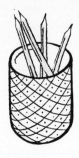

PENCIL
HOLDER

YOU WILL NEED:

> one soup can
> decorative paper, about 4 by 9 inches
> wall can opener
> soap; water; scrubbing brush; dish towel
> enamel paints
> scissors; glue; tape measure

MAKE IT LIKE THIS:

• 1. Open the soup with a wall-type can opener, so you won't have sharp edges on the can. Put the soup in a bowl. Your mother can use it for lunch or dinner.

• 2. Fill the sink with water and put the can in it. Let it stand in the water. The can label will come off easily after it has been soaked.

• 3. Remove the paper with your hands, soap the scrubbing brush, and scrub the inside and outside of the can thoroughly so no paper or smell of food remains on it. Dry the can well.

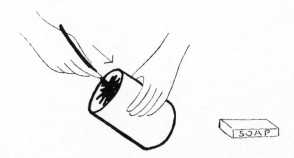

• 4. Paint the inside of the can with your favorite color paint. It will take a little while to get the can all covered with paint, so be patient, and wait for the paint to dry.

• 5. Spread glue evenly on the wrong side of the 4-by-9-inch piece of paper. Lay the can in the middle and cover it with the paper. If you have extra pencils around, sharpen them and put them in the can before wrapping the gift, which will be ideal for use on office desks, home writing tables, and next to the telephone.

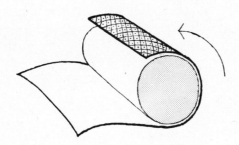

LETTER
FOLDER

YOU WILL NEED:

2 pieces of cardboard 8½ by 11 inches
a piece of decorative fabric 22 by 13 inches
2 pieces of plain white or colored paper 8½ by 11 inches
2 pieces of colored ribbon, each about 9 inches long
tape measure; rubber cement
thread; scissors; needle

MAKE IT LIKE THIS:

• 1. Hem the piece of fabric (see instruction No. 14, in the front), allowing one inch of fabric for each hem.

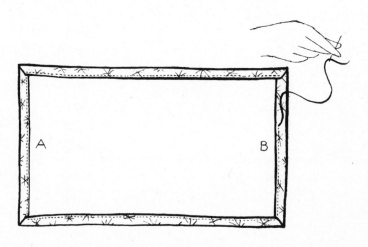

• 2. Cut one end of each of the ribbons on the bias and hem the other end. Sew one piece on each end of the fabric, in places marked **A** and **B**.

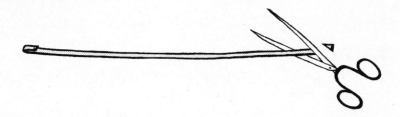

• 3. Glue the pieces of paper to one side of each of the pieces of cardboard.

• 4. Spread rubber cement on the fabric, but leave a 3-inch piece of fabric in the middle clear of glue. Glue the fabric to the sides of the cardboard which have not been covered with the paper. The unglued 3-inch strip of fabric in the middle will be the spine of the file.

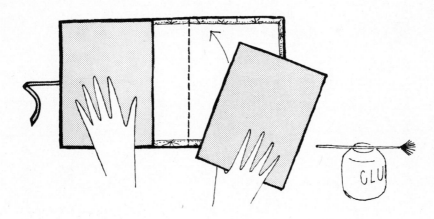

FAMILY CALENDAR

YOU WILL NEED:

a piece of cardboard 20 by 20 inches

12 pieces of white or colored construction paper, 14 by 17½ inches

family photograph or snapshot

decorative pictures for each month of the year, optional

ruler; crayons; paper punch

ribbon; scissors; mucilage or rubber cement

MAKE IT LIKE THIS:

• 1. Two inches from the top of the cardboard and in the middle of it paste on your family's photograph or snapshot.

• 2. Write the name of each of the twelve months of the year two inches from the top and in the middle of each of the 12 pieces of construction paper.

• 3. Since the piece of paper for each month is 17½ inches wide, you will have exactly 2½ inches in width to write the name of each day. Allow 2 inches in length from the spot where you wrote the name of the month. With your ruler and pencil

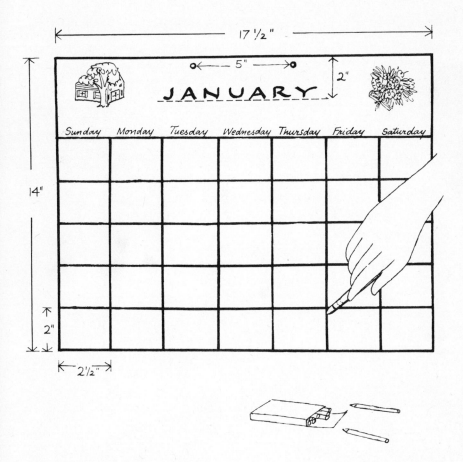

mark off dots that are 2½ inches apart. For the dates of the month you will need to mark off with the ruler dots that are 2 inches apart in the length of the paper.

• 4. Using a colorful crayon and ruler, draw lines to connect the places you marked. You will now have a box for every day of the month. Repeat this on each of the twelve pieces of paper.

• 5. Write the names of the days of the week in the boxes on top of every column and put in the dates by copying the days and dates from a printed calendar for the coming year. Write in with crayon, in the appropriate date boxes, the names of the people who have a birthday, anniversary, name day, or other celebration. Also mark national and local holidays, PTA meeting, sewing-circle days, bowling days, or whatever hobby your family participates in. If you wish, decorate the border of each month's sheet with magazine cutouts. Punch out two holes in the center of the cardboard, 5 inches apart and one inch from the top of the cardboard. Put a ribbon through and tie the ends.

This will be used for hanging the calendar on the wall. Punch out two holes, 5 inches apart and ½ inch from the top of the page, on the pages for each month. Pull a ribbon through each of the holes and tie in the back. Spread glue on the back of the last page and attach the whole thing to the cardboard, 5 inches from the top, one inch from the bottom and in the center. Write with crayons FAMILY CALENDAR on either side of the snapshot, and that's it.

• 6. This is sometimes called a Dutch calendar, and what a pleasant way of noting family events the people of Holland have invented!

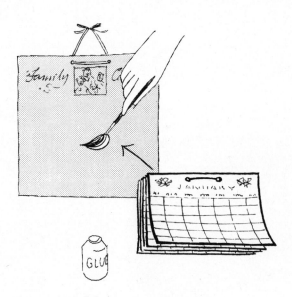

PLANTER

YOU WILL NEED:

    empty coffee can; dirt

    seeds for your favorite flower: marigold, morning glory, etc.

    12 to 20 pebbles, depending on their size

    black enamel paint; nail polish; brush; scrubbing brush; soap; water

Note: This present will take a few weeks to get ready.

MAKE IT LIKE THIS:

• 1. Wash the coffee can and let it dry. Paint the outside with black enamel paint. Let it dry and then paint it again. Then with nail polish copy the design on the illustration, either exactly as shown, or adapt it to your own taste. Remember what was said in the introduction about ingenuity!

• 2. Put the pebbles on the bottom and then fill the can with dirt and plant the seeds. Water the plant well every day for several weeks, but don't overwater it. When the seeds have sprouted and greenery shows it is ready to be given.

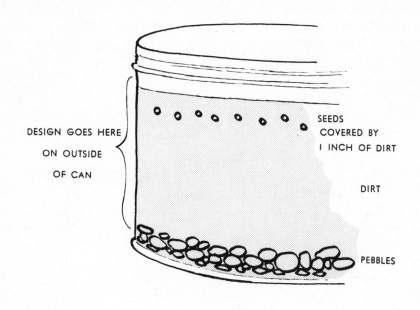

DESIGN GOES HERE
ON OUTSIDE
OF CAN

SEEDS
COVERED BY
1 INCH OF DIRT

DIRT

PEBBLES

REPEAT 3½ TIMES AROUND COFFEE CAN

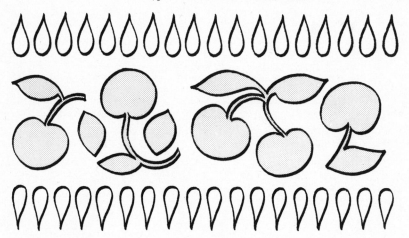

SHOE BAG

YOU WILL NEED:

> a piece of one-color fabric, 12 by 20 inches
> a piece of cord or tape about 25 inches long
> embroidery yarn; thread; needle
> scissors; tape measure; safety pin

MAKE IT LIKE THIS:

• 1. Hem one end of the fabric with a 1-inch hem (see instruction No. 14, in the front), which will be just big enough to pull the cord through.

• 2. At the point marked A on the illustration embroider 6 rows of chain-stitch lines (see instruction No. 11) for a decorative border. Use different color thread for each row.

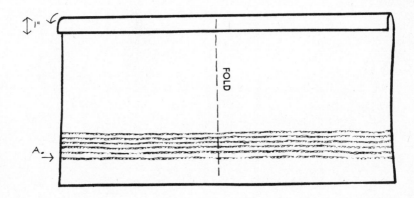

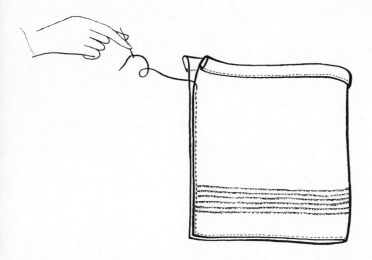

• 3. Sew together the sides, on the wrong side, with a backstitch (see instruction No. 7). Stop the sewing just below the place where you made the hem.

• 4. Attach the safety pin to one end of the cord and pull it through the hem. Tie the ends together. The cord is pulled tight to close the bag. This present is especially useful for someone who travels.

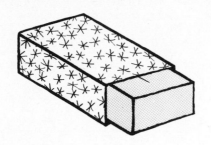

PAPER CLIP
HOLDER

YOU WILL NEED:

> large kitchen match box
> decorative paper
> rubber cement; show-card paint
> scissors; tape measure; brush

MAKE IT LIKE THIS:

• 1. Paint the part of the match box which held the matches and which will hold the paper clips when your gift is finished.

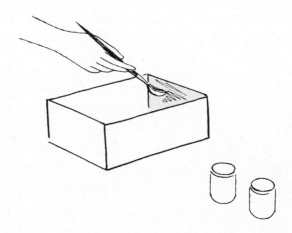

• 2. The cover of the match box should be decorated with pretty paper, oil cloth, or Con-Tact paper that you may have at home. All you need is a piece about 4¾ inches wide and 9 inches long. Spread glue on wrong side of the piece of decorative paper or fabric, place the match box cover in the center and bring the ends of the paper over to the top.

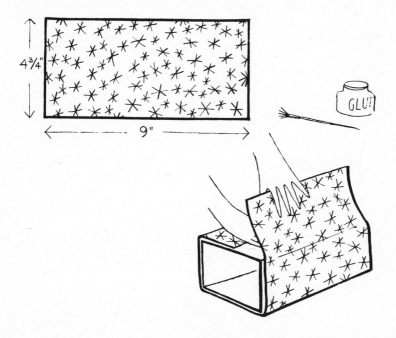

• 3. If you have money, buy a package of paper clips to put in the box, but even if you don't the kitchen match box turned into a lovely desk accessory will be a sufficiently pretty gift.

LETTER HOLDER

YOU WILL NEED:

> wire hanger; gummed tape

MAKE IT LIKE THIS:

• 1. Bend the hanger as indicated on the illustration.

• 2. Cover the wire with gummed tape so it is completely covered and looks pretty.

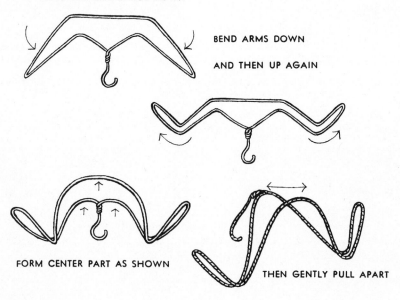

HOLD HANGER UPSIDE DOWN

BEND ARMS DOWN

AND THEN UP AGAIN

FORM CENTER PART AS SHOWN

THEN GENTLY PULL APART

BRICK
BOOK ENDS

YOU WILL NEED:

> 2 bricks
> scraps of felt fabric and decorative fabric
> shellac; glue; brush

MAKE IT LIKE THIS:

• 1. Dust all the surface dirt off the bricks. Cover the bricks with a coat of shellac. Let them dry.

• 2. Glue felt on sides A and B of the brick. These sides will

FELT FOR SIDES A AND B

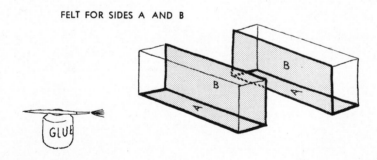

GLUE

touch the books and the bookcase and you will want them to be soft. On the other sides of the bricks glue any decorative fabric that you have. If you don't have scraps of fabric, use pretty paper.

One brick may be used as a door stop.

BOOK COVER

YOU WILL NEED:

> felt fabric, 21 by 9½ inches
> 14-inch piece of grosgrain ribbon
> wool yarn, matching or contrasting with the felt
> large-eyed needle and regular needle
> scissors; thread; tape measure

MAKE IT LIKE THIS:

• 1. Edge the whole piece of felt with long and short blanket stitches (see instruction No. 10, in the front), using the wool yarn and the needle with the large eye.

• 2. Fold over 3 inches at each end of the piece of felt so as to make it 15 by 9½ and sew the 3-inch edges with a backstitch (see instruction No. 7), using the regular needle and thread, in places A, B, C, and D, as indicated on the illustration. These folds will be used to slip in the book binding when the book cover is used.

• 3. Fold the cover in half to find the middle and at that spot sew on the piece of grosgrain ribbon, which will be used as a bookmark. Cut the unsewn end of the ribbon on a bias, so it won't shred.

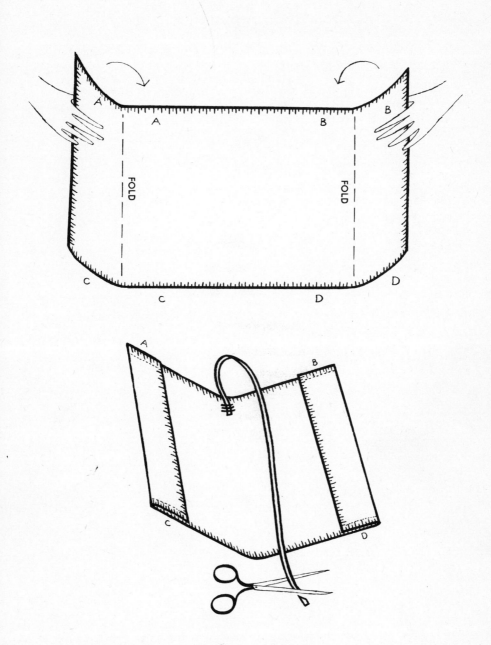

PAPERWEIGHT

YOU WILL NEED:

> large, smooth stone
> show-card or enamel paints
> brush; old newspapers

MAKE IT LIKE THIS:

• 1. Wash the stone and dry it *very* well. If stone has little pores and you can't reach them with a towel to dry, put the stone in the sun.

• 2. Spread old newspapers on your working surface. When the stone is completely dry, paint the stone all over with one color and let it dry.

• 3. Paint one of the designs shown on the opposite page (or your own) on top of the solid coat of paint and let it dry. (If your paint fails to stick to the surface of the stone, add a few soap flakes to the paint. That will make the paint stick.) A simple bean bag, with a pretty fabric cover, also makes a good paperweight.

CUFF LINKS

YOU WILL NEED:

> 4 buttons
> elastic thread
> scissors; tape measure

MAKE IT LIKE THIS:

• 1. Be sure that the buttons are not the kind with holes for sewing, but with a metal loop on the back.

• 2. Take a 3-inch piece of elastic thread and slip it through the metal loops of two buttons. Tie the two ends of the elastic thread together with two or three knots and cut off the ends, but not too close to the knot. Repeat this with the other two buttons and you have made a pair of cuff links. Easy as pie!

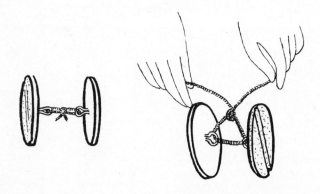

GIFTS FOR
CHILDREN AND
TEEN-AGERS

HEADACHE
BAND

YOU WILL NEED:

>1 yard of 1-inch velvet ribbon, any color
>
>6 small pearls or sequins, or 4 small mother-of-pearl buttons
>
>2 inches of 1-inch-wide elastic
>
>needle; scissors; tape measure

MAKE IT LIKE THIS:

• 1. Hem both ends of the ribbon (see instruction No. 14, in the front). Fold the ribbon like this.

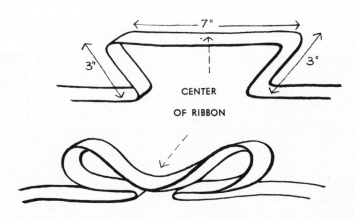

• 2. On the wrong side, sew with an overcasting stitch (see instruction No. 9) the two places where the ribbon has been folded.

• 3. Sew three little pearls or sequins or two mother-of-pearl buttons in a row at the places marked A and B.

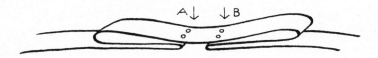

• 4. Sew the elastic to the hem marked D, and then bring the hem marked C to the other end of the elastic and sew that, too. Your headache band will be round and, because of the elastic, it will be adjustable to any head size.

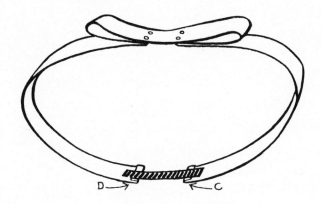

DECORATIVE
STATIONERY

1 package of 32 square envelopes

8 sheets of heavy 8½-by-11-inch paper (ask for sketching paper suitable for pen and ink)

scraps of felt fabric of assorted colors

glue; scissors; brush; pencil; tracing paper; pin

MAKE IT LIKE THIS:

• 1. Cut the 8½-by-11-inch sheets of paper into four parts (cut in half and then in half again), so you'll have 32 cards— enough for all the envelopes.

• 2. Trace the decoration shown on the opposite page onto the tracing paper. Cut it out and pin it onto the felt. Make each decoration in scraps of felt of two colors.

• 3. Cut out the felt according to the tracing on the paper. Put a little glue on one side of the felt and glue it onto the card in the upper left-hand corner. Repeat this until you have enough cards with decorations to fill all the envelopes. Pack the stationery in the box in which the envelopes came.

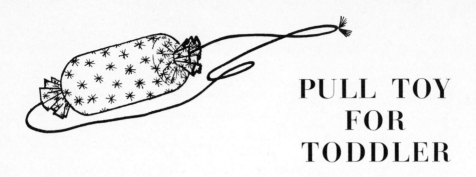

PULL TOY
FOR
TODDLER

YOU WILL NEED:

> empty cylindrical salt box or small oatmeal box
> ½ cup dry beans, or 12 small stones
> oilcloth or Con-Tact paper or other washable material
> long piece of cord
> two pieces of ribbon
> scissors; brush; glue; Scotch Tape
> nail and hammer; small safety pin

MAKE IT LIKE THIS:

• 1. Empty the box of all that was in it—be it salt or cereal. You've got to shake it thoroughly.

• 2. In the center of the top and bottom of the box, punch out a hole with the nail and hammer.

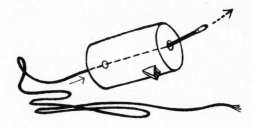

• 3. Attach small safety pin to one end of the cord and pull the cord through the two holes in the box, starting at the bottom.

• 4. Using the spout through which the salt was poured, put the dry beans or the stones into the box. Fasten down the spout with Scotch Tape.

• 5. Glue decorative oilcloth or fabric around the box-rattle.

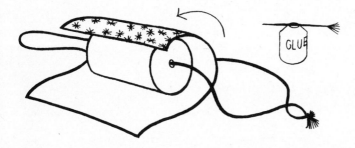

Gather the ends of the oilcloth or fabric at either end of the box and tie them with the ribbons. The rattle will look a bit like some party noisemakers, and any child who gets it will have a party and make noise!

MOBILE

YOU WILL NEED:

> 2 wire coat hangers
> gummed tape; ribbons; cardboard
> magazine cutouts
> show-card paints; scissors; glue; tape measure

MAKE IT LIKE THIS:

• 1. Straighten out the hook of one of the hangers. Cover both hangers with gummed tape. Slip one hanger through the other and wind the straightened hook around the other one.

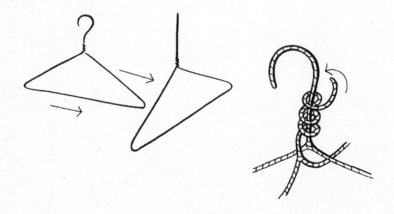

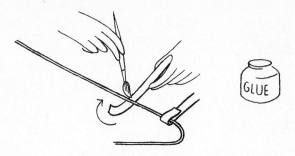

• 2. Glue on different lengths of colored ribbon every 3 inches on the wire hangers.

• 3. Cut out pictures that you like from magazines. Paste them on cardboard and cut the cardboard in the shape of the picture. Paint the side of the cardboard without a picture a solid color, with your show-card colors.

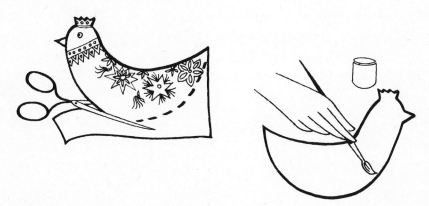

• 4. Glue the ends of the ribbons to the pictures and then when the mobile is hung somewhere the pictures will move as the air circulates.

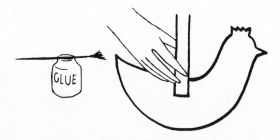

SCARF-BONNET FOR CHILD

¾ yard of fabric or two remnants
needle; thread; scissors; tape measure

MAKE IT LIKE THIS:

• 1. If you can do so, measure the child's head before cutting fabric (see how many inches it is from the tip of one ear to the other). If you don't know the size, make it as follows and it will fit a child of about 2 years.

• 2. Cut one piece of fabric to 14 by 14 inches and another to 7 by 30 inches.

• 3. Fold the 14-by-14-inch piece in half and sew on the wrong

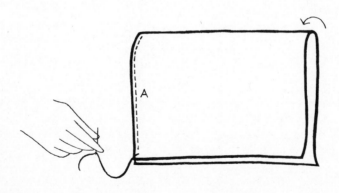

94

side the side marked A in the drawing. When turned inside out this will be the hat.

• 4. Fold the 7-by-30-inch piece of fabric in half lengthwise too. Sew it on the wrong side and turn it inside out. It will look a little bit like a tube, so press it with your hands against the side of a table to flatten it. This will be the scarf.

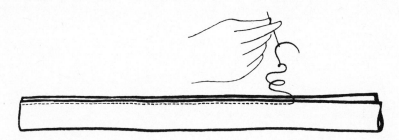

• 5. Sew the bottom part of the hat to the scarf part, leaving 1½ inches unsewn at the ends so it can be turned. It will look like a Dutch cap and keep the child warm.

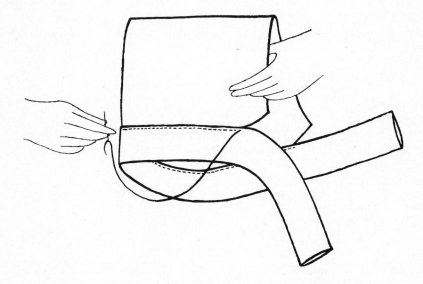

COLORFUL
SASH

YOU WILL NEED:

>   9 pieces of colored ribbon, each 9 feet long
>   needle; thread; scissors

MAKE IT LIKE THIS:

• 1. Take three pieces of ribbon and sew them together with a repeated cross-stitch at point A, indicated on the illustration. Point A is 3 inches from the beginning of the ribbon. Braid the three ribbons until you reach point B, 3 inches from the end of the ribbon. Sew the three ribbons together at this point. Repeat with the other six ribbons until you have three separate braids.

• 2. Sew all three braids together at the point marked A. Wind the three braids around one another about eight times and sew them at point marked B.

• 3. Cut the ends on the bias so they won't ravel. They will look like a pretty fringe.

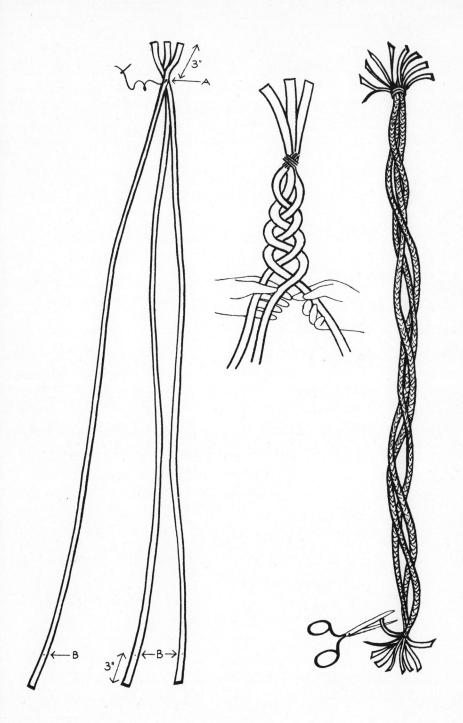

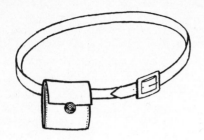

FELT BELT
WITH
CHANGE PURSE

YOU WILL NEED:

> a strip of felt fabric, 1½ by 28 inches and another
> piece of felt fabric 4 by 10 inches
> buckle, either from a worn-out belt or a new one
> button; needle; thread; scissors
> old paper; tape measure
> single-edged safety-razor blade

MAKE IT LIKE THIS:

• 1. Sew on the buckle at one end of the strip of felt fabric which will make the belt.

• 2. Fold the 4-by-10-inch piece of felt so that the purse itself will be 4 by 4 inches and the overlap, to close the purse, will be 2 inches. Sew sides A and B with a running stitch (see instruction No. 6, in the front) and at spot C make a loop with thread for the button (see instruction No. 18). Be sure the

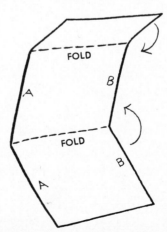

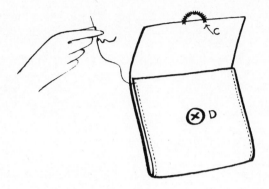

loop is big enough for the button, which you should sew on as marked (D) in the illustration.

• 3. Fold some old paper and put it in the purse, as flat as you can. Put the purse on a table, or other working place, with the back facing you. Using the razor blade, and doing this very carefully, cut two 1½ inch lengthwise slits ½ inch apart, ½ inch from the top of the purse. When you have done this, take the paper out of the purse.

BACK.

• 4. Slip the belt through the slits in the back of the purse and your practical gift is finished. Anyone riding a bicycle or carrying school books in both hands will welcome a belt which also has a purse.

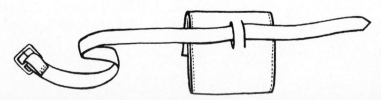

SCULPTURED
SOAP

square cake of white soap (the kind that floats is best) knife; tracing paper; pencil; pin

MAKE IT LIKE THIS:

• 1. Remove the brand name on the soap by scraping it off with your knife.

• 2. Trace the illustrations from these pages onto the paper. These are for the top, sides, and front of the soap. Put the paper on the proper sides of the cake of soap and make little pin pricks very close to one another to transfer the design from the paper to the soap.

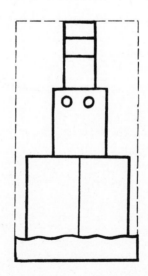

• 3. Carve away the soap around the design. Don't try to cut too much at one time, as cutting away a little piece at a time will get you results faster and easier. Don't try to cut it exactly on the line of the pin pricks. You can smooth out rough outlines later.

• 4. Run a little water over the soap figure and smooth out rough outlines of the design with your hands. After a minute or two of sculpturing the wet soap, the design should be nice and smooth and a plain piece of soap converted into a figure that will not only make a pretty gift, but will make the receiver of it clean as well!

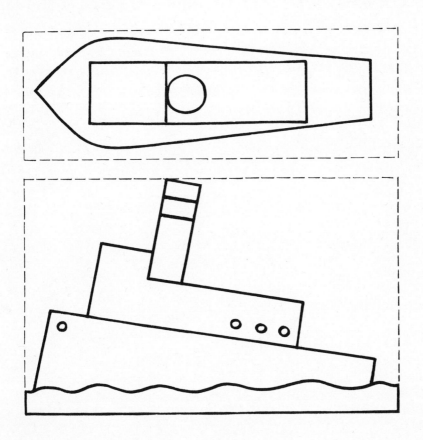

BROOCH

YOU WILL NEED:

> small scraps of felt or plush fabric
> cardboard; small button
> safety pin; thread; tracing paper
> pencil; pins; scissors; glue

MAKE IT LIKE THIS:

• 1. Trace the illustration of the flower onto your tracing paper. Attach the tracing paper to your scrap of fabric with a

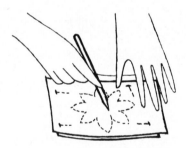

pin or two and cut the fabric along the pencil lines. Do this twice, so you have a piece of fabric for the front of the brooch and one for the back. Now cut the cardboard in the same shape as the fabric.

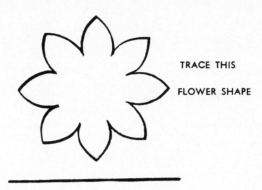

TRACE THIS

FLOWER SHAPE

• 2. Glue one piece of fabric onto the front of the cardboard, the other to the back.

FELT

CARDBOARD

FELT

• 3. Sew the decorative button in the center of the flower in the front and the safety pin, which will keep the brooch fastened to the dress of the wearer, to the back. Sew both the button and pin at the same time, using the same thread. That's all there is to that.

BACK

PONCHO

YOU WILL NEED:

1 large cotton or rayon challis scarf, bought inexpensively at 5-and-10
20½ inches of bias tape to match scarf
45 inches of ½-inch grosgrain ribbon to match scarf
scissors; tape measure; needle; chalk

MAKE IT LIKE THIS:

• 1. Fold the scarf so that it makes a triangle. Mark with chalk in the center of the scarf, on the folded line, a 10-inch strip and then cut a slit. This opening will be used for getting the head through.

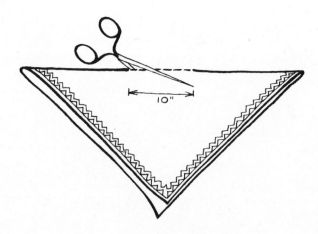

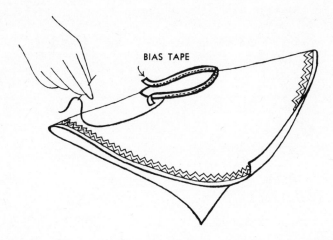

BIAS TAPE

• 2. Bind the slit with your bias tape, using a running stitch (see instruction No. 6, in the front).

• 3. On the wrong side of the scarf, at the tip of the triangle, make a 1-inch thread loop (see instruction No. 18). Cut the ends of the grosgrain ribbon on the bias and pull the ribbon through the loop. When the poncho is worn by the lady to whom you will give it, the ribbon will be used as a belt to hold the front and back in place.

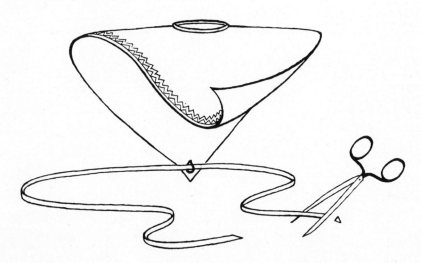

WALLET
BILLFOLD

YOU WILL NEED:

> 8½-by-10-inch piece of felt fabric
> wool thread to match or to contrast with felt
> large-eyed needle; scissors; tape measure

MAKE IT LIKE THIS:

• 1. Cut the felt into two pieces, one piece 8½ by 2½ inches and the other 8½ by 7½ inches.

• 2. Fold the 8½-by-7½-inch piece so that one part measures 8½ by 4 inches and the other 8½ by 3½ inches long.

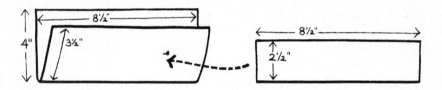

• 3. Put the 8½-by-2½ inch piece on top of the folded piece of felt. You will now have two separate pockets for money and papers.

• 4. Sew the felt wallet all around with an overcasting stitch (see instruction No. 9, in the front). Fold it in half and put a heavy book on top of it for a few hours to make it hold a wallet shape. Then it is done.

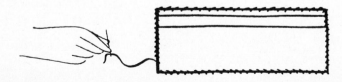

FLOWER
BARRETTE

YOU WILL NEED:

> 3-inch-long steel barrette from 5-and-10
> 5 wool flowers (see directions for making these on page 46)
> scissors

MAKE IT LIKE THIS:

• 1. Make five colorful wool flowers by following the directions.

• 2. Using the pieces of wool that serve as stems for the flowers, tie them on securely to the upper part of the barrette, one close to another. This will look pretty on a teen-age girl, or younger child.

APPLE-SHAPED
PAJAMA
CASE

YOU WILL NEED:

> red felt fabric
> green button
> green wool thread
> scissors; large-eyed needle

MAKE IT LIKE THIS:

• 1. Cut the felt into two circles 18 inches in diameter. The circles must not be absolutely perfect in roundness, for no apple is ever absolutely round, is it? Cut out a triangle with curved sides, 8 inches long on each side, from each circle.

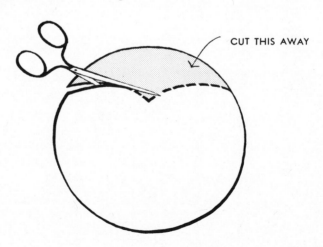

CUT THIS AWAY

• 2. Sew the circles together with a blanket stitch (see instruction No. 8, in the front) except for the place where you cut out the triangle. Use the green wool thread for sewing.

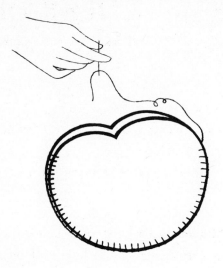

• 3. In the center of the triangle sew on a button on one side and a large green wool thread loop on the other side (see instruction No. 18). This will look a little like the stem of an apple. The pajama case will look "delicious," just like a good apple.

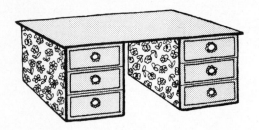

DOLL'S CHEST OF DRAWERS

YOU WILL NEED:

> 6 empty match boxes; cardboard, 8 by 4¾ inches
> decorative paper; 6 buttons
> show-card paint; glue; scissors; tape measure

MAKE IT LIKE THIS:

• 1. Glue three match boxes one on top of the other. Do the same with the other three match boxes. These will be for the drawers of the doll chest.

• 2. Glue decorative paper all around the two separate sets of match boxes. Paint the ends of the inside parts of the match boxes the same color as you will paint the cardboard for the top of the chest.

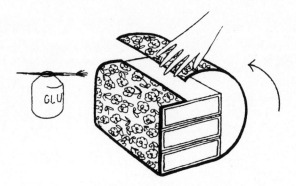

• 3. Paint the cardboard a color either matching or contrasting with the decorative paper. Glue it on top of the match boxes. There will be 3 inches between the two sets of match boxes.

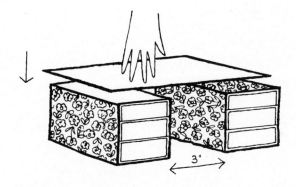

• 4. Glue on pretty buttons, or beads, as indicated in the illustration, and your chest of drawers will be finished.

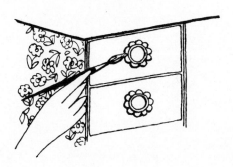

KIMONO NIGHTSHIRT FOR A BABY

YOU WILL NEED:

>1½ yards of flannel or cotton fabric
>20 inches of ribbon to match fabric
>thread to match fabric; embroidery yarn
>brown wrapping paper, or other clean paper
>tape measure; scissors; needle; small pins; pencil

MAKE IT LIKE THIS:

• 1. Enlarge the paper pattern for the kimono nightshirt by following instructions on the diagram. Use a sheet of paper about 22 by 22 inches. The length of the kimono should be 20 inches, the width from the edge of one sleeve to the edge of the other sleeve also 20 inches, and the width of the kimono directly under the armhole 14 inches. Then cut out the paper pattern.
• 2. Pin your pattern on top of the fabric and cut the fabric to the same size and shape as the pattern. You will need one piece for the back and one for the front of the shirt. Cut the fabric for the shirt front in half.

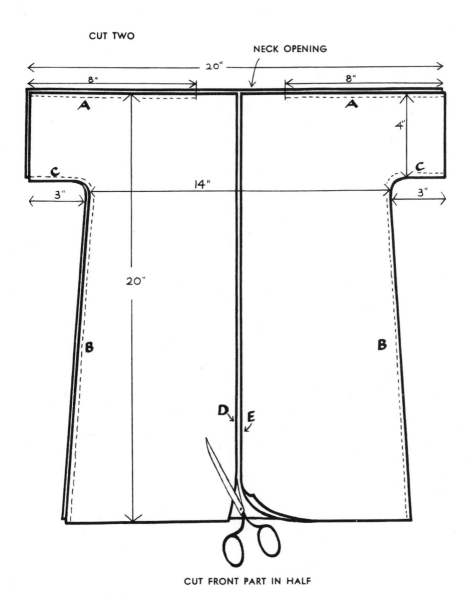

CUT TWO

NECK OPENING

20"

8"   8"

A   A

4"

C   C

3"   14"   3"

20"

B   B

D   E

CUT FRONT PART IN HALF

113

• 3. Sew sides marked A, B, and C with a backstitch (see instruction No. 7, in the front). Hem the bottom, the neckline, the front parts, marked D and E, and the sleeves of the shirt.

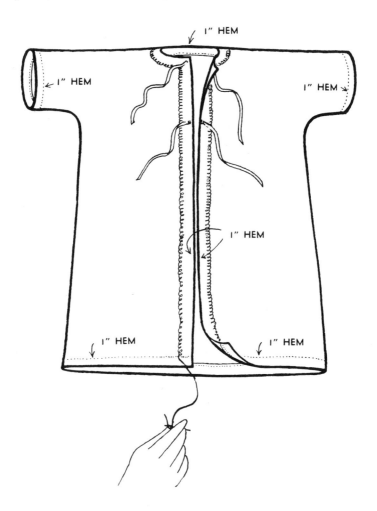

• 4. With your embroidery yarn sew a chain-stitch border at the neckline and in the front of the kimono shirt. Sew on 5-inch pieces of ribbon at the neckline and 4 inches down from the neckline. Cut the ends on the bias and that's all!

GIFTS FOR
THE WHOLE
FAMILY

CHRISTMAS TREE ANGEL

YOU WILL NEED:

> white construction paper
> tracing paper
> small piece of gold ribbon
> blue and gold paints
> pencil; paper punch; scissors

MAKE IT LIKE THIS:

• 1. Transfer the angel pattern given here onto your tracing paper. Cut it out and then put the pattern on top of the white construction paper and cut the construction paper into the same shape.

• 2. Color the angel's dress with blue paint, the wings and head with gold paint, and leave the face and hands white. Use the pencil, or black india ink if you have it, to mark the eyes and mouth of the angel.

• 3. Punch out a small hole at the top of the angel's halo and pull through the ribbon for hanging the angel at the top of the Christmas tree.

CHRISTMAS TREE
CHAIN

YOU WILL NEED:

> construction paper: red, green, white, and gold
> narrow ribbon of any color; glitter
> tracing paper; glue; pencil
> scissors; paper punch

MAKE IT LIKE THIS:

• 1. Trace the patterns for the star, bell, and ball onto your tracing paper. Cut them out of the tracing paper.

• 2. Put the patterns you have made on your construction paper and cut out as many stars, bells, and balls as you can.

• 3. At the tip of each bell and ball, punch out a small hole with the paper punch for the ribbons to go through. Make a small hole in the corner of one of the points of the star, also with your paper punch.

• 4. Put a little glue on in the center of the balls and bells and along the edges of the five points of the star. Sprinkle the glitter in the places where you put the glue and let it all dry well. Shake off the excess glitter. Turn the balls, bells, and stars around and do the same on the other side, putting glue and then glitter in the places suggested.

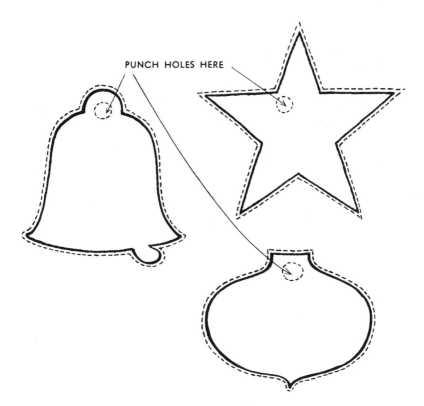

PUNCH HOLES HERE

• 5. Pull the ribbon through the holes you have made in the various decorations. First pull the ribbon through a star, then through a bell, then through a ball, and then again through a star until you have all your decorations strung up on the ribbon. It will be a mighty fine Christmas tree chain, all glittery and bright.

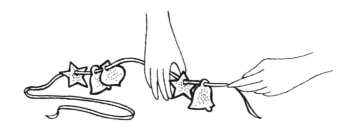

YARN-SPOOL
CHRISTMAS TREE
DECORATIONS

YOU WILL NEED:

> empty yarn spools
> enamel paints, different colors
> beads, sequins, pearls, or glitter
> narrow ribbon
> brush; scissors; old newspapers

MAKE IT LIKE THIS:

• 1. Remove the paper labels from the ends of the spools. Spread old newspapers on your working surface and paint the spools all different colors.

• 2. Before the paint has completely dried, press small beads or sequins carefully onto the spools, or sprinkle the wet paint with glitter. When the paint dries you will find it served also as glue, because the beads, sequins, or glitter will stay attached to the spools. If for some reason they don't, let the paint dry completely and then glue on the pretty sparklers.

• 3. Pull pretty ribbons through the holes in the spools and tie the ends. These spools will look very bright as they hang on the branches of your Christmas tree.

OLD-FASHIONED CHRISTMAS TREE CHAIN

YOU WILL NEED:

> colorful pages from magazines
> scissors; glue; ruler; pencil

MAKE IT LIKE THIS:

• 1. Cut out as many full-color pages as you can from various magazines. Using the pencil and the ruler mark the pages into ½-inch-wide strips. Cut out these strips, then cut the long strips into 4-inch lengths.

• 2. Put a little glue on the end of one of the ½-by-4-inch strips and bring the other end over and glue them together, so the paper forms a circle. Slip another strip of paper through this circle and glue it together too. Continue doing this until you have a chain about 60 inches long. It doesn't cost a penny and looks lovely on a Christmas tree.

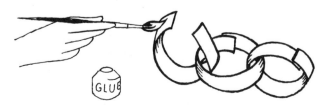

SHOE-SHINE
CLOWN

YOU WILL NEED:

scraps of felt fabric, one about 8 by 5 inches, another
5 by 5 inches
wool yarn in color contrasting with the felt
chalk; large-eyed needle; scissors; tape measure

MAKE IT LIKE THIS:

• 1. Cut the larger piece of felt (marked A on the picture) into
an oval shape for the botton of the shoe-shine clown. Cut one
end of the smaller piece of felt (marked B on the picture) into
an oval shape for the face of the clown.

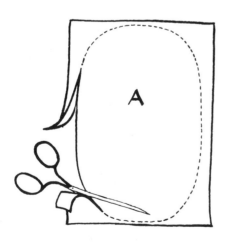

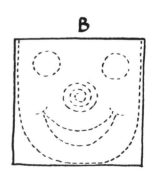

• 2. Draw with chalk on the smaller piece of felt the place where you will later embroider eyes, eyelashes, nose, and mouth. Using the outline stitch (see instruction No. 12, in the front) embroider over the chalk the features of the clown.

• 3. Put the piece of felt on which you embroidered the face on top of the larger piece of felt and sew them together with an overcasting stitch (see instruction No. 9). At the top of the "head" sew a large loop (see instruction No. 18) with your wool yarn and your shoe-shine clown is ready. It will be ever so useful in your father's office closet, or at home in the hall closet or shoe-shine box.

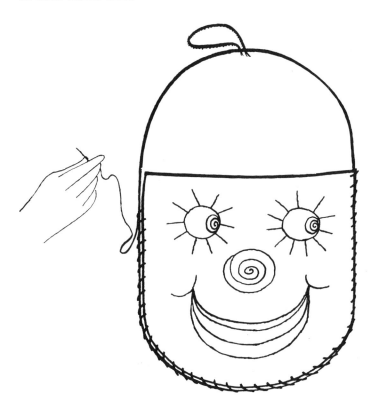

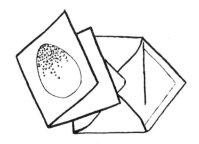

HANDMADE
EASTER
CARDS

YOU WILL NEED:

> 6 sheets pink, yellow, or blue construction
>   paper, about 8½ by 11 inches
> 12 square envelopes
> yellow, blue, lavender construction paper
> tape measure; tracing paper
> colored crayons; pencil; scissors

MAKE IT LIKE THIS:

• 1. Cut the six sheets of paper in half. Fold these 12 pieces in half so that each card is 4¼ by 5½ inches.

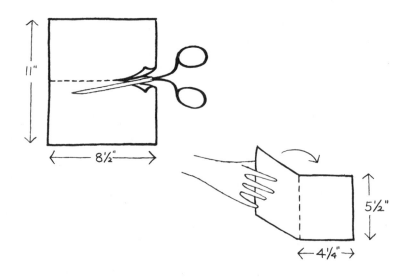

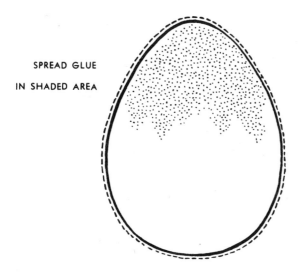

SPREAD GLUE
IN SHADED AREA

• 2. Trace the illustration of the Easter egg. Then put the tracing paper on the other pieces of paper and cut out twelve Easter eggs. Paste one in the center of each card.

• 3. Put a little glue on top of the Easter egg and sprinkle a little glitter in the places where you put the glue. Let it dry and then shake off the excess glitter.

• 4. Write your Easter message with colored crayons inside the card, and put one card under the flap of each of the envelopes. Wrap them in a gift package and send them out at least a month before Easter. On the package write OPEN BEFORE EASTER!

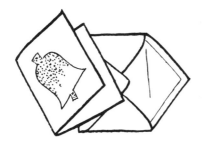

HANDMADE CHRISTMAS CARDS

YOU WILL NEED:

12 sheets white paper 8½ by 11 inches

24 square envelopes

green and red construction paper

a package of glitter; red nail polish

tape measure; tracing paper; pencil; scissors

MAKE IT LIKE THIS:

• 1. Cut each sheet of paper in half. Fold the 24 pieces of paper in half so that each card is 4¼ by 5½ inches.

• 2. Trace the illustrations of the Christmas tree, the bell, and the tree ornaments onto the tracing paper. Then put the tracing paper on the construction paper, and cut out eight Christmas trees, eight bells, and eight tree ornaments. Paste one in the center of each card.

• 3. Put a little glue on top of the Christmas tree, the tree ornaments, and the Christmas bell. Sprinkle the glitter in the places where you put the glue. Dry and shake off the extra glitter.

• 4. Write your Christmas message with nail polish inside the card. Let it dry, then put one card under the flap of each of the envelopes. Wrap them in a gift package and send them out at least a month before Christmas. On the package write OPEN BEFORE CHRISTMAS!

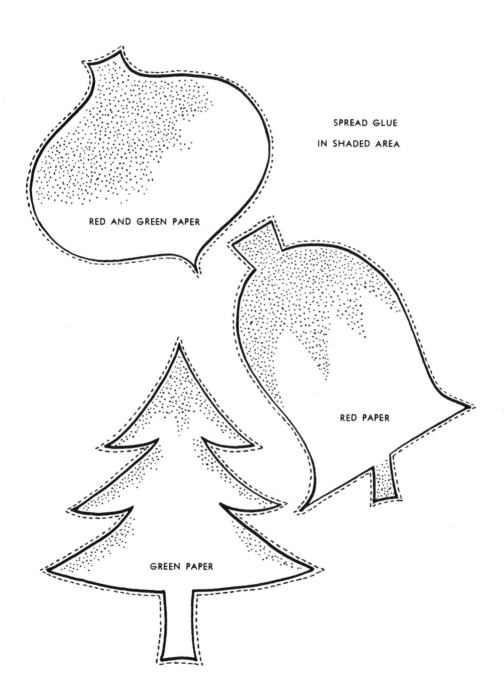

SPREAD GLUE
IN SHADED AREA

RED AND GREEN PAPER

RED PAPER

GREEN PAPER

HANDMADE
VALENTINE
CARDS

YOU WILL NEED:

>6 sheets pink construction paper 8½ x 11 inches
>12 square envelopes
>red construction paper
>12 small white doilies
>red nail polish
>tracing paper; tape measure; pencil; scissors

MAKE IT LIKE THIS:

• 1. Cut each sheet of pink paper in half. Fold the 12 pieces of paper in half so that each card is 4¼ by 5½ inches.

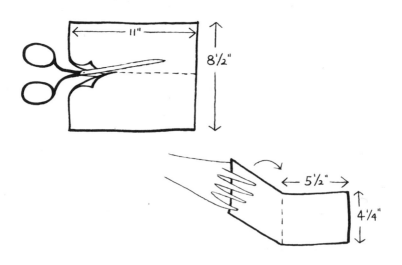

• 2. Trace the illustration of the heart. Put the tracing paper on the construction paper and cut out twelve red hearts.

• 3. Paste one heart in the center of each doily and then paste a doily with the heart on it on top of each pink card. ·

• 4. Write your St. Valentine's Day message with nail polish inside the card. Let it dry, then put one card under the flap of each of the envelopes. Wrap them in a gift package and send them out about three weeks before St. Valentine's Day and mark the package OPEN BEFORE ST. VALENTINE'S DAY!

COOKIE JAR

YOU WILL NEED:

> 1 large (3-pound) empty Crisco or Spry shortening can
> enamel paints; brush for painting
> soap; water; scrubbing brush

MAKE IT LIKE THIS:

• 1. Scrub the container with soap and hot water so that no left-over traces of shortening or smell remain. Peel all the paper from the outside of the can and scrub off all the left-over bits with the brush and soap.

• 2. Paint the whole can, including the cover, a solid color. You'll have to repeat this two or three times until no tin shows.

• 3. When the solid paint has dried, paint a design over it, following as closely as you can the design shown here. You can also paint designs shown on pages 147, 151, 155, 158, and 168. That's all.

REPEAT THIS DESIGN

SPICE JARS

YOU WILL NEED:

> 6 empty large wide-necked medicine bottles or baby-food jars (with screw-on tops or plastic covers)
> red nail polish or enamel paints
> paint brush; soap; water

MAKE IT LIKE THIS:

• 1. Wash all the bottles or baby-food jars very carefully and scrub off all the paper labels.

• 2. Paint stripes on the bottle with the red nail polish. Also with the nail polish write the names of the spices on the plastic covers of the bottles: Paprika, Oregano, Pepper, Cinnamon, Marjoram, Tarragon. If you use the metal tops of the baby-food jars, you will have to paint over the printing first with a solid color. Then write the names of spices with nail polish. A set of these jars makes a mighty handsome, and useful, gift.

ODDS-AND-ENDS
BAG

YOU WILL NEED:

> 2/3 yard of denim fabric 36 inches wide
> red bias tape; thread to match
> scissors; tape measure; needle

MAKE IT LIKE THIS:

• 1. Fold the piece of denim fabric so it is 18 by 24 inches. Make

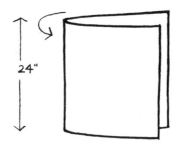

an 8-inch slit on one side of the fabric and bind it off with the piece of red bias tape (see instruction No. 15, in the front).

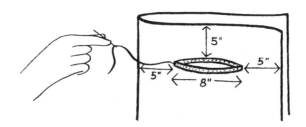

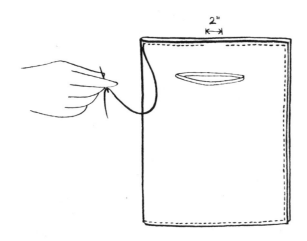

• 2. Sew three sides, except for a 2-inch portion in the middle, on the wrong side with a backstitch (see instruction No. 7) and turn it inside out. The 2 inches left unsewn will be used for the hook of the hanger to go through.

• 3. Put the hanger through the large slit and pull the hook of the hanger through the 2-inch slit. Then the bag is finished and it can be used on the inside of a closet door, in the bathroom, or in any part of the house where you want odds and ends kept in order.

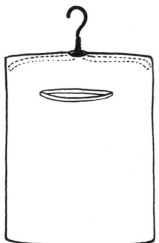

PAPIER-MÂCHÉ
BOWL

old newspapers, paper toweling, napkins
glue; shellac; Vaseline; show-card paints
glass bowl; single-edged safety-razor blade

MAKE IT LIKE THIS:

• 1. Shred newspaper into strips about 3 or 4 inches long and about 1 inch wide.

• 2. Put the bowl upside down on a piece of newspaper on the table or on the floor. Put a thin layer of Vaseline all over the bowl. Glue the strips of paper all over the bowl, crisscrossing the strips one on top of another. Repeat this until you have 12 layers of paper strips.

• 3. Let the paper dry completely. It will take a whole day. Then cut off the edges all around the bowl, using the razor blade. Gently take off the papier-mâché form from the glass bowl and wipe off any traces of Vaseline from the inside of the form.

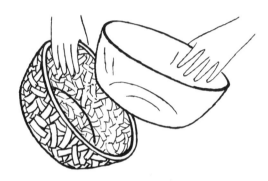

• 4. Paint the outside and then the inside of the papier-mâché bowl a solid color and let it dry, and then paint a design on top on the inside and outside of the bowl with contrasting paints. When all the paint has dried, put a coat of shellac on top of the paint, for a permanent finish. This can be used for pretzels, potato chips, hard candy, and other dry goodies.

MINIATURE
SHADOW BOXES

YOU WILL NEED:

> 3 to 6 shallow cans—such as sardine, tuna fish, sprats
> enamel paints
> evergreens or sea shells and pebbles, etc.
> 3 to 6 glue-on picture hooks
> wall can-opener; brush; glue; Saran wrap
> soap; water; gummed tape

MAKE IT LIKE THIS:

• 1. Discuss this project with your mother and ask her to save the cans for you; or ask when she plans to serve sardines or a tuna salad or casserole and then open the cans. Assuming you have the problem settled of what is going to be done with the perfectly fine food, proceed like this:

• 2. Wash the cans thoroughly with soap and water. Dry them well.

• 3. Paint the cans all over with the enamel paint, in your favorite color—pale green if you make an evergreens design, pale pink or blue if you make a sea-shell-and-pebble design. Let the paint dry.

• 4. Decide on pretty arrangements of evergreens or pebbles and sea shells for the 3 to 6 cans. See the illustration for ideas. After you've decided how to arrange the decorations, glue them on the bottoms, inside the cans.

• 5. Cover the cans with Saran wrap. Put gummed tape around the edges of the cans.

• 6. Attach the gummed picture hooks to the backs of the cans. When the miniature shadow boxes are hung in a pretty arrangement on the wall of the person to whom you'll give this interesting gift, you will see that all your work was well worth the effort.

GUEST
TOWELS

YOU WILL NEED:

½ yard 45-inch-wide white cotton fabric
white thread; colored thread
scissors; tape measure; needle

MAKE IT LIKE THIS:

• 1. Cut the fabric into four 11-by-18-inch pieces. Hem each piece (see instruction No. 14, in the front).

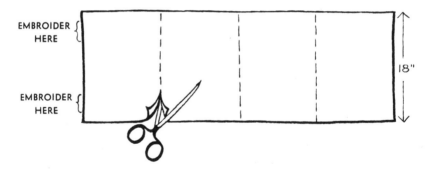

• 2. Make a border on each end of the towel by embroidering three rows of a chain-stitch pattern (see instruction No. 11), each in a different color thread. Red, green, and yellow are nice, and so are pink, purple, and light blue.

• 3. Repeat this on all four towels and you have an elegant gift for any holiday or celebration.

THROW PILLOW

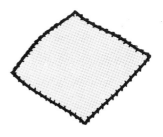

YOU WILL NEED:

> 2 pieces of seersucker or flannel fabric about 15 by 15
> inches
> 12 pairs or more of old nylon stockings
> thread to match fabric
> thread contrasting in color with the fabric
> needle; scissors; tape measure

MAKE IT LIKE THIS:

• 1. Place the pieces of fabric together so that the wrong sides are on the outside. Sew them together on three sides with a backstitch (see instruction No. 7, in the front). Turn this case inside out. The side which you did not sew will be used as an opening through which to put the nylon stocking "filler."

• 2. Cut the nylon stockings into small pieces.

• 3. Put the nylon pieces in the pillow case. Sew the open side with a small running stitch (see instruction No. 6).

• 4. To decorate the pillow sew an overcasting stitch with the thread of contrasting color all around the edges (see instruction No. 9). This pillow can be easily washed in any washing machine and is perfect anywhere in the house.

SEA-SHELL
SHADOW BOX

YOU WILL NEED:

> top of shoe box
> a selection of sea shells
> pale pink or pale green paper
> gummed tape to match paper
> glue-on picture hook; Saran wrap
> Duco cement; scissors; tape measure

MAKE IT LIKE THIS:

• 1. Line the inside of the top of the shoe box with the pink or green paper.

• 2. Try different arrangements by moving the sea shells around and when you have found an arrangement you like, cement the sea shells on. Be careful not to put too much cement on the backs of the sea shells and not to break them. Let the box stand a while until the cement has dried.

• 3. Take a piece of Saran wrap about 5 inches longer than the length of the shoe-box lid. The Saran wrap paper is just about right in width for an average shoe box cover. When you are sure that the shells are securely cemented to the inside of the lid put it upside down in the center of the Saran wrap and bring the Saran wrap over to the back of the lid. Saran wrap stays in

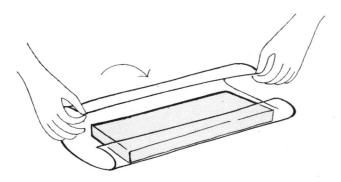

place when you press it gently, so press it down to the box and fold the corners as you fold paper corners when you wrap a present. Glue the gummed tape on the edges of the shoe-box top, so it looks like a frame.

• 4. On the back, glue on the gummed picture hook and your shadow box is ready for wrapping.

WALL
NAPKIN
HOLDER

YOU WILL NEED:

> 2 glazed-surface paper plates, 6-inch or 8-inch size
> scraps of wool yarn or ribbons
> pictures of fruit or flowers, or anything you like, cut out
>   of magazines
> paper napkins
> scissors; pencil; large-eyed needle
> paper punch; rubber cement (glue)

MAKE IT LIKE THIS:

• 1. Cut one of the paper plates in half with the scissors. Put the half plate on top of the whole plate and hold both lightly with your fingers.

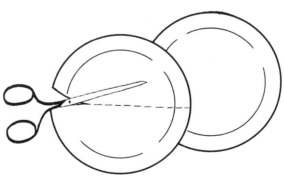

• 2. With tape measure and pencil make small dots every inch, as shown on the illustration, and punch out holes in the spots that you marked with pencil.

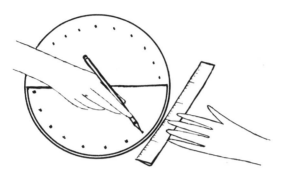

• 3. Use wool yarn to sew the half plate onto the whole plate by winding it through the holes and making a loop in the center hole of the whole plate to hang it on.

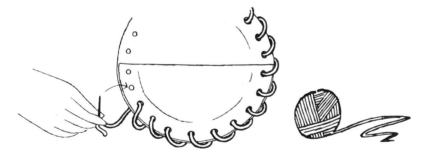

• 4. Glue the cut-out pictures from the magazine onto the half plate to decorate the holder and fold about eight to ten multicolored, or white, paper napkins and slip them into the holder as shown in the illustration.

GREETING CARD DISPLAY HANGER

YOU WILL NEED:

> wire coat hanger
> scraps of ribbons, any color
> gummed tape; glue; scissors; tape measure

MAKE IT LIKE THIS:

• 1. Put gummed tape all over the hanger so that the wire does not show anywhere.

• 2. Have 15 to 20 ribbons of varying lengths—from 15 to 36 inches. Glue them on the hanger, both on the upper and lower parts, about 1 to 2 inches apart. These will be used to pin on, or glue on, Christmas cards, or birthday cards, or whatever. The hanger can be displayed on a picture hook anywhere in the house.

"PATCHWORK QUILT" TOY BOX

YOU WILL NEED:

> empty carton; brown wrapping paper
> leftover pieces of colorful wrapping paper, or full color
>   pages from a weekly magazine
> scissors; tape measure; glue
> shellac; brush

MAKE IT LIKE THIS:

• 1. Ask at your local supermarket, grocery store, or other shop for an empty carton. Measure and then cut a piece of brown wrapping paper to fit the inside of the box. Glue it onto the inside of the box.

• 2. To decorate the outside of the box you can use any leftover pieces of gift paper or colorful pages from different magazines. Glue the paper in patchwork-quilt fashion—every which way: one page a bit on top of the other, upside down and sideways. Put shellac all over the box and let it dry.

• 3. Such a box can be used for keeping toys in place, for storing blankets, or keeping workshop utensils in order.

PLACE MATS

YOU WILL NEED:

> 2/3 of a yard of 36-inch-wide fabric, either butcher linen, denim, or Indian Head muslin
> one skein each of yellow, white, and green embroidery yarn
> thread to match your fabric
> scissors; tape measure; needle
> pencil; pins; tracing paper

MAKE IT LIKE THIS:

• 1. Cut the fabric into four 18-by-12-inch pieces. Hem the individual pieces (see instruction No. 14, in the front).

• 2. Trace the design of the daisy bouquet shown in the illustration four times onto your tracing paper. Cut the piece of tracing paper so that you have four 5-by-5-inch pieces of paper, each with the daisy bouquet on it.

• 3. Pin the design onto the upper right-hand corner of each piece of fabric, about 3 inches from the hem.

• 4. To embroider the design, use the white yarn for the petals, yellow for the centers, and green for the stems. To make the petals of the flowers use chain stitch (see instruction No. 11), but return the needle to the center of the flower. Use outline stitch (see instruction No. 12) with green yarn for the stems of the flowers.

• 5. When the design is completely embroidered on each place mat, take out the pins holding the tracing paper in place and tear it off very gently. This gift takes more time to make than many of the others in this book, but the effort and time you'll devote to it will be worth the result. Next time you can make a set of napkins to go with the place mats, using the same kind of fabric and embroidering a daisy bouquet in the corner of each napkin.

PRESSED-FLOWER PICTURE

3 or 4 flowers

5 or 6 leaves of various shapes

8½-by-11-inch double sheet of plastic (the kind used in loose-leaf notebooks)

gummed tape; glue-on picture hook; Duco cement

heavy book; tissue paper

MAKE IT LIKE THIS:

• 1. Collect the flowers for pressing. Daisies, poppies, corn-flowers, pansies, and other field flowers press well. Then get half a dozen leaves that go well in size and shape with the flow-

TISSUE PAPER

ers. Put the leaves and flowers between two pieces of tissue paper and then between two pages of a heavy book. Put the book flat on a table and put other heavy books on top of it.

• 2. When the flowers are dry (after about four weeks) you can start arranging them for the picture. Open the double sheet of plastic and with tiny little drops of cement attach the flowers and leaves to the back sheet of the plastic. Put the other sheet of plastic on top.

• 3. Use the gummed tape to make a "frame" around the plastic and attach the gummed picture hook as close to the top edge as possible.

FLOWER VASE

> milk bottle or other bottle with a wide top
> enamel paint (any color but red); brush
> red nail polish

MAKE IT LIKE THIS:

• 1. Wash and scrub the bottle. Let it dry. Paint the outside with any color enamel paint and let it dry.

• 2. When the enamel paint has dried, make the design shown in the illustration with nail polish. You can use two different shades of red (and iridescent white nail polish if you wish). Use one, two or all three sections of the suggested design on the bottle, depending on the size of the bottle. Let it dry and the vase is finished.

151

KITCHEN
OR
BATHROOM
CURTAINS

YOU WILL NEED:

> 1½ yards of polka-dotted cotton fabric 54 inches wide
> (white polka dots on a yellow background is pretty)
> white embroidery yarn
> white or yellow thread
> needle; scissors; tape measure; thimble

MAKE IT LIKE THIS:

• 1. Measure the window for which you plan to make the curtains. The standard kitchen window is about 70 by 35 inches, and a bathroom window is about 60 by 27 inches. Let us assume that yours are of this size.

• 2. We'll make a top valance for the window 8 inches long by 35 inches wide, and a one-piece café curtain for the bottom of the window, 35 by 35 inches. Of course, you must allow enough material for hems and gathering, so the piece of fabric for the valance will actually be 13 inches long and 54 inches wide. The piece for the bottom part will be 40 by 54 inches.

• 3. Make a 1-inch hem (see instruction No. 14, in the front) on one end of the piece of valance fabric and on the piece of the café curtain fabric. On the other ends of both pieces make 3-inch hems. After you have made the 3-inch hems, sew a running stitch 1 inch from the top.

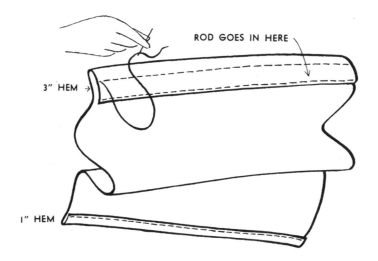

ROD GOES IN HERE

3" HEM →

I" HEM

• 4. On the ends where you have the 3-inch hems, between the running stitch and the hem, the curtain rods will be pulled through.

• 5. To make a flower border for the kitchen curtains, make chain-stitch petals (see instruction No. 11) around every other polka dot on the bottom of the valance and café curtain parts. Repeat this on the second row of polka dots, also embroidering every other polka dot.

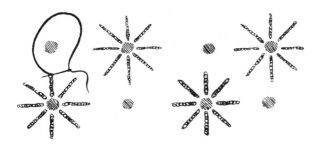

• 6. Fold the curtains carefully and pack them in a box.

EMBROIDERED PICTURE

YOU WILL NEED:

> a piece of linen, butcher linen, or denim fabric, 10 by 13
> inches
> thread to match the fabric
> embroidery yarn—green, yellow, red, or other color
> a round wooden stick, 8 inches long and not more than
> ½ inch in diameter
> 15 inches of ribbon
> 2 thumb tacks; pins; needle
> scissors; tracing paper; pencil

MAKE IT LIKE THIS:

• 1. Hem sides marked B, C, and D with a 1-inch hem. Hem
side marked A last with a 2-inch hem (see instruction No. 14,
in the front).

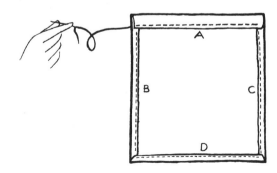

• 2. Trace the illustration onto your tracing paper. Pin the tracing to the center of your piece of fabric.

• 3. Embroider the vase with green yarn with an outline stitch (see instruction No. 12), and the flowers with yarn of different colors and a chain stitch (see instruction No. 11).

• 4. When your embroidering is all done, take out the pins and tear the tracing paper off ever so gently.

• 5. Slip the wooden stick into the 2-inch hem and with thumb tacks attach the ribbon to the ends of the stick. The ribbon will be used for hanging up this wall tapestry.

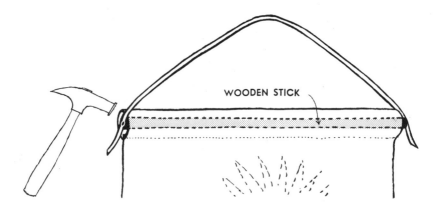

WOODEN STICK

COASTERS

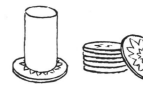

YOU WILL NEED:

a piece of cardboard
show-card paints—green, white, and yellow
shellac
can, glass, or small bowl about 3 inches in diameter
pencil; scissors; brush; emery board or sandpaper

MAKE IT LIKE THIS:

• 1. Put can, glass, or small bowl on top of the cardboard and trace with pencil 6 (or 12) circles. Cut them out with the scissors and smooth the sides with the emery board.

• 2. Paint the disks green. Let the paint dry. Then look at the illustration and as closely as possible make the same picture on each cardboard circle. Let the paint dry.

• 3. Put shellac all over the top and let it dry. This will prevent the coasters from becoming soggy when water glasses are put on them.

YELLOW

WHITE

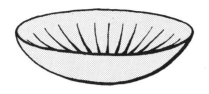

DECORATIVE
BOWL

YOU WILL NEED:

> small wooden bowl, either old or new
> poster paints—blue and yellow
> clear shellac or varnish; brush; old newspapers

MAKE IT LIKE THIS:

• 1. Spread old newspapers on your working surface so that you don't make it dirty with your paints. Paint the bowl all over with blue paint. Let the paint dry and then give the bowl another coat of blue paint. Let the second coat of paint dry too.

• 2. Paint the sunburst with yellow paint. Let the paint dry.

SUNBURST
MOTIF

• 3. Put a coat of clear shellac, or varnish, over the entire bowl. Let it dry and give the bowl another coat of shellac or varnish. Such a pretty bowl can be used for candy, potato chips, or other goodies and it is a useful and thoughtful gift.

CANAPÉ HOLDER

YOU WILL NEED:

piece of Styrofoam, 10 inches square or round
yellow show-card paint; knife; pencil
colored toothpicks

MAKE IT LIKE THIS:

• 1. Draw lightly on the piece of Styrofoam the illustration shown here. Cut away with a knife, carefully and slowly, the excess pieces of Styrofoam. When you have finished cutting, you will see that the Styrofoam looks something like a daisy.

• 2. Make a little circle with the yellow paint in the middle of your piece of Styrofoam and then your flower will be complete.

• 3. Stick in the colored toothpicks every inch or so, all over the Styrofoam flower. They will be used when the receiver of this gift serves little sandwiches with tea or coffee when friends come visiting.

TOASTER COVER

YOU WILL NEED:

    fabric scraps, two pieces of patterned fabric 10 by 7½ inches each, and one piece of solid-color fabric 25 by 6½ inches

4 inches of ribbon

scissors; tape measure; needle; thread

MAKE IT LIKE THIS:

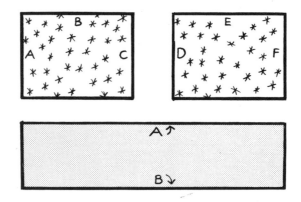

• 1. The long solid-color piece of fabric will be for the top of the toaster and the two smaller, patterned pieces will be for the sides. Sew sides A, B, and C of one of the small patterned pieces of fabric to side A of the long piece of fabric. Then sew sides D,

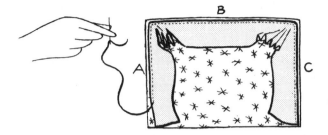

E, and F of the other small patterned piece of fabric to side B of the long, solid piece. Use a backstitch (see instruction No. 7, in the front) and do your sewing on the wrong side of the fabric.

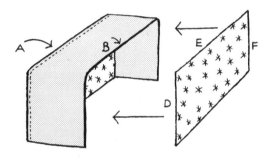

• 2. When all the sides are sewn together, hem the toaster cover (see instruction No. 14). Turn it inside out. In the center of the top of the toaster cover sew on your piece of ribbon which you folded like a loop. Be sure that the toaster is not warm or plugged in when you put the cover on.

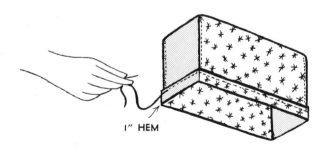

1" HEM

SMALL BRAIDED RUG

YOU WILL NEED:

rags of all colors and sizes
scissors; needle; thread; tape measure

MAKE IT LIKE THIS:

• 1. Cut your rags into 1-inch strips. You will need three strips to make a braid. Make each strip as long as possible by sewing together many rags, but all three strips should be of equal length for easy braiding. The length of the strips of rags, and therefore the length of your braid, will determine the size of your rug. To make the braid longer, you can sew on more strips as you braid.

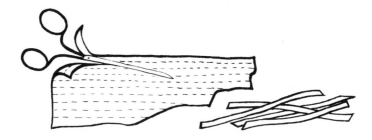

• 2. Sew together the three rag strips at one end. Put this end

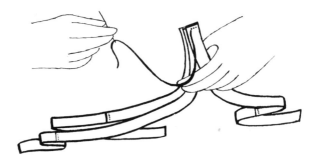

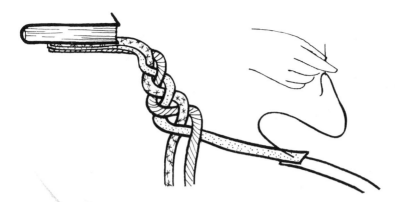

on a chair and put a very heavy book on top of it. Then start braiding the rags.

• 3. When you have 25 inches of braid ready, start coiling it. As you wind the braid round and round, sew it with an overcasting stitch (see instruction No. 9, in the front). Continue braiding the rags and sewing the braid until you have no more rags and the rug measures approximately 25 to 30 inches in diameter. Sew the last inch of rags, unbraided, on the side of the rug which will be next to the floor. This rug will look pretty in a foyer, by the bedside, or in the bathroom.

WOVEN
TABLE
RUNNER

YOU WILL NEED:

wool thread of two contrasting colors (red and blue,
red and orange, yellow and blue, or blue and green)
heavy cardboard, 10 by 20 inches
large-eyed, blunt needle; pencil; scissors

MAKE IT LIKE THIS:

• 1. Use a pencil to make marks ¼ inch apart along each 20-inch side of the cardboard. Then cut little notches at these marks.

• 2. Wind a piece of wool all around the cardboard so it goes into the notch on one side and then through the corresponding

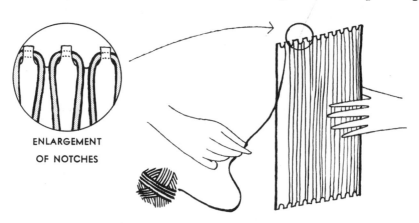

ENLARGEMENT
OF NOTCHES

notch on the other. Tie the ends of the wool in the back of the cardboard. These threads are called warp threads.

• 3. Put the other color wool in the needle and weave it over and under each of the strands of yarn you have wound around the cardboard. This thread is called a weft thread. Use the side of the needle to move one row of the wool you are weaving close to the next.

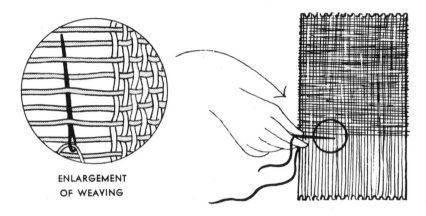

ENLARGEMENT
OF WEAVING

• 4. When you are finished weaving, cut the warp wool threads in the back of the cardboard.

• 5. Take several warp threads together and tie them. They will become a pretty fringe to a runner that can grace any bureau or table in your or your friend's home. If you want to make the fringe shorter, cut off a little of the ends.

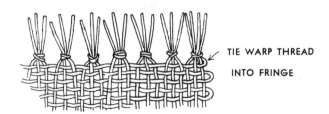

TIE WARP THREAD
INTO FRINGE

KITCHEN MEMO PAD

YOU WILL NEED:

heavy cardboard, 8½ by 11 inches
white paper pad, 5 by 7 inches
poster paints—red and black
small picture from magazine
elastic string; decorated Band-Aid
scissors; pencil; paper punch; 10 inches of ribbon
tape measure; glue; brush

MAKE IT LIKE THIS:

• 1. Paint the cardboard with the red paint. Let the paint dry. With the black paint, letter the words DO NOT FORGET at the top of the cardboard. Let the paint dry.

• 2. Paste the pad of paper onto the cardboard, as shown.

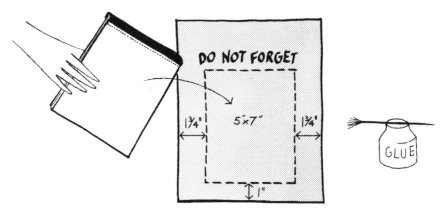

• 3. Tie one end of the elastic thread around the pencil, one inch from the top. Put the plastic Band-Aid around the elastic thread and the pencil, to hold it in place.

• 4. Put glue on the back of the small picture you cut out of a magazine and paste it over the other end of the elastic thread in the upper right-hand corner of the cardboard.

• 5. Punch two holes at the top of the cardboard, 4 inches apart. This will make each hole 2¼ inches from the edge of the cardboard. Pull the ribbon through these holes and tie the ends together. The ribbon will be used for hanging the reminder pad on a hook in the kitchen, dinette, or office of the person who will receive this present.

DAISY TRAY

cookie-baking sheet, old or new
poster paints—green, white, and yellow
clear shellac or varnish
brush; old newspapers

MAKE IT LIKE THIS:

• 1. Spread old newspapers on your working surface, so that you don't make it dirty with your paints. Paint the baking sheet all over with green paint, first on one side and then on the other. Let the paint dry and then give the tray another coat of green paint on both sides. Let the second coat of paint dry.

• 2. Paint the flower petals white, the centers yellow. Let the paint dry. Other designs are on pages 130, 147, 151, 155, 158.

• 3. Put a coat of clear shellac or varnish over the entire tray to protect the surface when it is used. Let the shellac or varnish dry completely and then put on another coat of shellac or varnish. Let that dry too and your gift is ready.

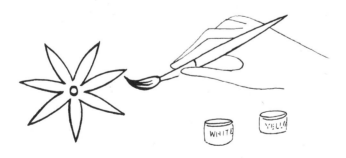

GOOD THINGS
TO EAT

CRANBERRY-ORANGE RELISH FOR THANKSGIVING AND CHRISTMAS

YOU WILL NEED:

2 large cans whole cranberry sauce

2 fresh, seedless, oranges

1 package orange gelatin

1½ cups hot water

measuring cup; large mixing bowl

mixing spoon; knife; can opener

2 large jars

MAKE IT LIKE THIS:

• 1. Empty the package of orange gelatin into the mixing bowl. Add 1½ cups of hot water and stir the gelatin until it has dissolved. Let it cool.

• 2. Open the cans of whole cranberry sauce and add the cranberry sauce to the gelatin mixture.

• 3. Peel the oranges and remove all you can of the white pith. Cut the oranges into small pieces and add them to the cranberry-gelatin mixture.

• 4. Ladle the sauce into two jars and you will have two delicious gifts to give to two families for Christmas or Thanksgiving. It's perfect with turkey.

CHOCOLATE-CEREAL CANDY

YOU WILL NEED:

>6-ounce package of semisweet chocolate morsels
>2 cups of any dry cereal: Rice Krispies, corn flakes, etc.
>4 tablespoons light corn syrup
>1 tablespoon water
>double boiler; measuring cup and measuring spoons
>wooden spoon; teaspoon; wax paper
>cookie sheet, or other flat pan or board
>white paper doily; box to hold candy

MAKE IT LIKE THIS:

• 1. Half-fill the bottom part of the double boiler with water and bring it to a fast boil. Be careful when you do that. Remove from stove burner. In the top part of the double boiler, put in the corn syrup, water, and chocolate morsels. Stir this with a wooden spoon until the chocolate has melted, and the whole thing looks like a syrup.

• 2. Stir in slowly the two cups of dry cereal and see to it that every cereal bit is covered by the chocolate syrup.

• 3. Put a piece of wax paper on top of the cookie sheet or wooden board. Using a teaspoon, drop little pieces of the candy-coated cereal on top of the wax paper. Chill for about two hours in the refrigerator or other cool place. Remove the candy carefully from the wax paper and then put it on top of a paper doily in a tin or cardboard box and your gift is ready for giving and eating.

BOX OF
CHOCOLATE
MARSHMALLOW
CANDY

YOU WILL NEED:

1 package instant chocolate pudding

1 pound confectioners' sugar

1 egg white

2 tablespoons milk or cream

1/3 cup butter

1/3 cup marshmallow cream

large mixing bowl; measuring cup

measuring and mixing spoons

large piece of wax paper

rolling board; rolling pin; knife

paper doily and old chocolate box

MAKE IT LIKE THIS:

• 1. Empty the instant chocolate pudding powder into the mixing bowl. Add 1 pound confectioners' sugar.

• 2. Pour 2 tablespoons milk or cream over the sugar and pudding. Add one egg white. (To separate egg white from egg yolk do this: Crack the egg over a bowl or a teacup and let the white drip into it. Put the egg yolk into the small jar and cover it with one tablespoon of cold water or milk to keep it from drying out. Cover the jar and put it into the refrigerator. Perhaps it can be used by Mother.) Mix the sugar and the pudding with the milk and egg white.

• 3. Measure 1/3 cup butter (about ¾ of a stick of butter) and put the cup with the butter into a bowl of warm water from the tap. Let the butter melt a little. Don't melt it entirely, just soften it a bit.

• 4. Add the softened butter to the bowl with the pudding and sugar mixture. Mix it with the spoon for about three minutes. Then wash your hands well and dry them. Using your hands, knead (mix) the pudding and sugar mixture until it becomes doughy. It should take about three or four minutes to do this.

• 5. Put the large piece of wax paper on the rolling board. Sprinkle a little confectioners' sugar on the wax paper and put the candy dough on the wax paper. With the rolling pin, roll out the candy dough until it is about ¼ inch thick. If the candy dough sticks to the rolling pin, sprinkle some confectioners' sugar on top of the dough. Try to roll it into a square shape, not a round one. Cut the candy dough into five strips, each 1½ inches wide.

• 6. Spread four of the strips with marshmallow cream (it comes in jars) and pile them one on top of the other. Do not spread the fifth strip. Put it on top. Wrap the candy in the wax paper on which it was rolled and put it into the refrigerator for about three hours. Handle the candy very carefully when you are putting it into the refrigerator so that you do not break it.

• 7. When the candy has hardened, take it out of the refrigerator and put it back on the rolling board. Open the wax paper wrapping. Cut the candy strip into ¼-inch slices. Have a candy box, or other tin or carton box you have around the house, right near you and put the paper doily in it. As you cut the candy put it on the doily and you are ready. It's fun to make this candy and it looks good and tastes delicious.

A GIFT
OF COOKIES

YOU WILL NEED:

1 cup shortening, or butter

2 cups sugar

2 eggs

4 tablespoons milk

4 teaspoons baking powder

1 teaspoon vanilla extract

$\frac{1}{4}$ teaspoon salt

4 cups flour

2 large mixing bowls; measuring cup

measuring and mixing spoons

rolling board; rolling pin

cookie baking sheet

cookie cutters

doily; box of any kind

MAKE IT LIKE THIS:

• 1. Save out one tablespoon of butter. Put the rest, together with the sugar, milk, eggs, and vanilla extract into a mixing bowl and mix it well with a spoon.

• 2. Mix almost all of the flour (leave a little for dusting the rolling board when you roll out the dough), the baking powder, and salt in the other bowl. Mix it well also.

• 3. Put the mixed flour, baking powder, and salt in the bowl with the butter, sugar, milk and egg mixture. Wash your hands extremely well. Knead the dough in the bowl until all the ingredients are well mixed. Put the dough into the refrigerator for one to two hours.

• 4. Take the dough out of the refrigerator and put it back on the table. Tear smaller pieces away from the big piece of dough and roll them out on the rolling board, always dusting the breadboard a little, so the dough doesn't stick to it. When the dough is about $1/8$ inch thick, or even less, start cutting out cookie shapes with your cutters. (If you don't have cookie cutters, use a glass to make round cookies.)

• 5. Light the oven and set the temperature for 375 degrees. Wait 10 or 15 minutes for the oven to heat up. Grease the cookie sheet all over with a little butter and put the cookies on it. Leave about $1/2$ inch between cookies. Put the cookie sheet in the oven and continue rolling out dough so that when one batch of cookies is done you will have more ready to put on the cookie sheet. The cookies bake in about 10 minutes, but do see that they are nice and tanned, not too brown, when you take them out of the oven. Be careful with the hot cookie sheet; use a pot holder in each hand all the time.

• 6. When your cookies are all finished and have cooled, put them in boxes and wrap them for gift-giving. You will have enough for three or four plentiful gifts.

ICE CREAM PIE

YOU WILL NEED:

> 12 graham crackers
> 1 tablespoon sugar
> ¼ cup (⅛ pound) butter
> 1 package strawberry gelatin
> 1 cup hot water from the tap
> 1 pint strawberry ice cream
> ½ cup heavy cream
> 1 tablespoon confectioners' sugar
> measuring cup; measuring spoons
> 2 mixing bowls; mixing spoon
> 8-inch pie pan; rotary beater; aluminum foil

MAKE IT LIKE THIS:

• 1. Melt the butter by putting the cup with the butter into a bowl of hot water from the tap.

• 2. With your hands (be sure that they're clean), crush the graham crackers into tiny pieces and crumbs. You should have about 1 cup of crumbs. Put the crumbs and the tablespoon of sugar into one of the mixing bowls.

• 3. Add the melted butter to the crackers. Mix together with a spoon.

• 4. Line the bottom and the sides of the 8-inch pie pan with the cracker-and-butter mixture.

• 5. Open the package of strawberry gelatin and put the gelatin powder into the other mixing bowl. Add 1 cup hot water from the tap. Stir until the gelatin dissolves. When the gelatin has melted, add 1 pint of strawberry ice cream to it and stir until the ice cream has also melted. Let the mixture stand for 5 minutes. Then beat the ice cream and gelatin mixture with the rotary beater for 5 minutes, so that it becomes light and fluffy.

• 6. Pour the gelatin and ice-cream mixture into the pie pan lined with the graham cracker crumbs. Cover with aluminum foil and put into the refrigerator for at least 4 hours before serving.

• 7. Just before serving, or wrapping it as a gift, whip ½ cup heavy cream with 1 tablespoon confectioners' sugar until the cream is stiff. Put the whipped cream on the pie and wrap again in aluminum foil if you have to carry it to someone as a present. If you give it to your mother and father, you don't need to wrap it, just slice it and serve it!

RAISIN CHOCOLATE CLUSTERS

YOU WILL NEED:

6 or 7 ounces semisweet chocolate morsels
1 cup of seedless light or dark raisins
double boiler; hot water
cookie sheet, wooden board, or flat tray
wooden spoon; teaspoon; measuring cup
wax paper; paper doily; box

MAKE IT LIKE THIS:

• 1. Fill the bottom part of the double boiler half full with hot water. Put the upper part of the pot on the bottom part. Put the chocolate morsels in the upper part of the pot and stir with wooden spoon until the chocolate has melted and become syrupy.

• 2. Add a cup of raisins to the chocolate syrup and stir them until they are all covered with the chocolate syrup.

• 3. Put wax paper on top of a cookie sheet, wooden board, or tray. With the teaspoon drop little clusters of chocolate-covered raisins onto the wax paper. Put in the refrigerator to chill for about 10 hours. When chilled and hardened, put them on top of the paper doily in a metal or wooden or cardboard box. You will have about 2½ dozen delicious candies to give your family or friends.

CHOCOLATE FROSTED ANGEL CAKE

YOU WILL NEED:

2 3-ounce packages cream cheese
1 tablespoon milk
2½ cups confectioners' sugar
2 tablespoons chocolate syrup; 1 teaspoon vanilla
8-inch unfrosted angel food cake
measuring spoons; measuring cup
mixing bowl; mixing spoon; spatula
wax paper; 9-inch paper doily; scissors
cake platter, or box

MAKE IT LIKE THIS:

• 1. Put the cream cheese into the mixing bowl. Add 1 tablespoon milk and blend it into the cream cheese with the spoon. Gradually add the 2½ cups confectioners' sugar and mix until the cheese and the sugar are well blended.

• 2. Add 2 tablespoons chocolate syrup, and 1 teaspoon vanilla. Stir again until everything is well mixed.

• 3. Put the angel food cake on the piece of wax paper. With the spatula, spread the cream cheese mixture smoothly over the cake, covering the top and sides. When the cake is all covered, put the paper doily on the cake platter or in the cake box. Lift the cake carefully with the wax paper and put it on the platter. With the scissors cut off the wax paper around the cake.

• 4. Chill the cake in the refrigerator for at least 3 hours, and then present it to your family or to your friends.

APRICOT
PIE

YOU WILL NEED:

> 1 1-pound can apricot halves
> 12 lemon snaps
> ¼ cup (⅛ pound) butter
> 1 tablespoon brown sugar
> 1 package instant vanilla pudding
> 1¼ cups of milk
> can opener; sieve
> 2 large bowls; 1 small bowl
> clean dish towel; wooden mallet or small hammer
> measuring cups; measuring spoons
> 9-inch pie pan; wax paper; rotary beater

MAKE IT LIKE THIS:

• 1. Open the can of apricot halves and put the apricots into the sieve over a large bowl. Drain off all the syrup.

• 2. Crush the lemon snaps into tiny pieces and crumbs. Here is an easy way to do this: Place the snaps on one half of a clean dish towel. Fold the other half of the towel over the snaps. Pound gently with a wooden mallet or small hammer until all the snaps are crushed. You should have about one cup of crumbs. Put them into the small mixing bowl.

• 3. Put ¼ cup butter into a cup. Place the cup in a bowl of hot water from the tap. Be sure the water does not get into the cup with the butter.

• 4. When the butter is soft add it to the cracker crumbs and mix well.

• 5. Press the mixture of crumbs and butter into the pie pan covering the bottom and sides of the pan.

• 6. Put the apricot halves, round side up, on top of the cracker crust. The number of apricots you will have will just about cover the bottom of the pie pan. Sprinkle the apricots with 1 tablespoon brown sugar.

• 7. Open the package of vanilla pudding and put the pudding powder into a large mixing bowl. Slowly add 1¼ cups milk, mixing the pudding powder and the milk with the rotary beater until the pudding is smooth.

• 8. Pour the pudding over the apricots in the pie pan, and cover with wax paper. Put into the refrigerator to chill for three hours. Then it will be just right for giving to someone when you go visiting.

ABCDEFG
HIJKLMN
OPQRSTU
VWXYZ

abcdefghijklm
nopqrstuvwxyz
1234567890

ABCDE
FGHIJK
LMNO
PQRSTU
VWXYZ

Index

About the Author

Esther Hautzig's familiarity with books for boys and girls is a result, perhaps, of three points of view; for she is a parent, an author, and an active participant in the publishing and promotion of children's books. *Let's Make Presents* is her second book; the first, *Let's Cook Without Cooking*, was written under her maiden name, Esther Rudomin.

Mrs. Hautzig inherited from her mother, a former arts and crafts teacher, a love of making things out of materials around the house. In relating the background of this book, she writes, "My family of cousins, near and distant, was enlisted to test my directions with their children and their friends. The directions were found easy!"

Born in Vilno, Poland, Mrs. Hautzig subsequently lived in Siberia; Lodz, Poland; and Stockholm, Sweden. She came to this country as a young girl and studied at Hunter College before entering the publishing field. She has traveled extensively in Europe, Israel, and Mexico and now resides in New York City with her husband, a well-known concert pianist, and their young daughter, Deborah.

About the Artist

Ava Morgan studied art at Cooper Union and now designs and illustrates books. She is married to Alfred Weiss, a chemical engineer, whose work often takes them throughout the United States and Europe. When they are not traveling, Mr. and Mrs. Weiss live with their two sons in New Jersey.